INTRODUCTION

I've been working in the com
since the late 90s, back in th
considered a good connectic
phones were executive toys
How times have changed.

If there's one thing that I could share from my
experience it would be this: communications isn't an
industry, it's what we do in our everyday lives. That's
why this book isn't about technology, it's about
people. If we want to understand mobile technology
and its bright future, we need to first appreciate the
stories of those changing it right here today. And that
starts with the youth.

I spent the best part of a decade traveling the world on
a quest to find these stories and I'm excited to be able
to share some of them with you here, in this book.

This wouldn't have been possible without the support
of those around me who have been very helpful, and
understanding of this journey. So, thanks to my
colleagues and researchers: Josh Dhaliwal, Ghani
Kunto, Freddie Benjamin, Maha Hafeez, Binbin Lu and
Everaldo Aguiar. And a special thanks to my editor,
Maxine Garcia, whose patience and eye for detail made
this possible.

Graham Brown

CONTENTS

1 ANHUI, CHINA

In the early hours of Friday April 29 2011, 17 year old high-school student Xiao Zheng returned to his family's apartment in Anhui province in Eastern China. Without disturbing his sleeping mother, he crept into his room, placed a dusty travel bag beside his unmade bed and fell into a deep sleep.

Less than a year later, Zheng was lying in a hospital bed, lethargic and short of breath, fighting for his life as his body slowly shut down with organ failure.

As the local media unraveled Zheng's story, a picture of modern China began to emerge. On the surface, the Zhengs were like any other aspirant Chinese family. They had uprooted themselves from their home town in search of better prospects in a bigger city. They had made sacrifices and often spent months living apart. But as every unearthed nugget of evidence helped build a clearer picture of what really happened to Xiao Zheng that day, journalists and audiences alike were less interested in the details and more in why it happened.

Anhui may have had its fair share of vices, but Zheng was a good kid who few would have gravitated towards trouble.

and trends?

It's easy to see Mobile Youth as the story of a generation of digital natives defined by an obsessive relationship with technology that rewrites the social rulebook and "ruins everything". But this isn't the story I want to tell. I want to tell the untold story. This is the "why?" story the media often fails to address. Perhaps what youth like Xiao Zheng really want isn't mobile phones and iPads, but the analogue existence that has been lost in the rampant march towards progress: hanging out in a friend's bedroom, playing with cousins in the park or something as simple as the touch of a hand. The rise of technology isn't undermining the social fabric of society. Technology's rise is a response to our loss of a meaningful social world.

2 HACHIKO EXIT, SHIBUYA JAPAN

The US outranks Japan 50:1 when it comes to the number of domestic lawyers, even though Japan is only half its size. In Japan, this is called wa, or as we know it, harmony. It's the social code that prioritizes belonging over the need to stand up for your individual principles. Following the 2011 Touhoku earthquake, journalists visiting Japan were astonished by the absence of looting when the desperation on the broken streets was juxtaposed with the wealth of consumer gadgetry in the vacant stores. But wa is not all good. Wa means sucking it up and not saying what you really think. Wa means a teenage girl will remain silent as a pervert feels her up whilst roaming the crowded subway train taking "upskirt" photographs.

Here, at the Hachiko Exit at Shibuya Station, Tokyo is a sea of humanity adhering to the principles of harmony. I came here nearly 20 years ago in search of a future that lay in the miracles economies of the East; a young graduate, full of optimism and curiosity, wanting to see what lay beyond the hole in the fence. It was the mid–1990s and the beginning of the communications revolution that, by the end of 2010, would put one billion mobile phones into the hands of the world's youth. Here is where I learned that this revolution isn't the domain of technology, but of people. Communications isn't an industry, but what people do on a day-to-day basis.

Amongst the waves of people dressed in muted tones spilling out into the light from the airless underground are mottled clusters of vivid pink and yellow. Girls in loud jackets and improbably high platform heels gather round a small mobile phone screen, concealing their laughs with orange-tanned hands. For some, this is just a sea of people milling around a narrow, crowded concourse with convenient stainless steel ash stands and topiaries dressing the border. For me, however, and those curious about the unwritten code of human behavior, this is an insight into the social nature of mankind. This is communication, yet the industry that makes $400 billion a year from the world's under 30s knows little about how it works.

Guided safely by the unfailing mechanical heartbeat of the electronic clock, the million-strong army of multi-colored ants moves from the concourse and waits patiently by the Hachiko crossing. Advertisers have precisely 30 seconds to blast their messages at the audience staring up at the 20-meter high screens. A voice extols the virtues of CC Lemon, a sugary beverage with 50 times the recommended daily allowance of vitamin C. The messages are occasionally drowned out by the ubiquitous auto-tuned J-Pop harmonies cascading from above or by the chorus of an arriving subway train, never late, chiming its two-bar melody. I read that if you added together the two-bar melodies of all the stations on the central Yamanote line you could form a complete musical score.

As the lights change, eager shoppers, gaggles of excited high school girls and time-pressed salarymen begin to move on cue as if engaged in a performance for the Olympic opening ceremony. They have 60 seconds to traverse the infamous "X" crossing. The clock ticks:

55...54...53...

The crowd begins to thin. Stragglers pick up the pace.

40...39...38...

They speed up their march, following a consumerist pheromone trail up the hill towards the Marui and Isetan department stores.

25...24...23...

A lone cyclist wearing pristine white gloves and a surgical facemask brings up the rear.

2...1...0.

The lights turn green and a mass of cars once again reclaims the crossing. The cycle begins again.

Every day, more than four million people, or the entire population of Los Angeles, pass through this strip of concrete, no more than 100 meters in width. With admirable orchestration, they pour out of the world's busiest station, part of the world's busiest mass transit system, into the world's biggest city.

50% of the world's mobile-owning youth live in Asia. But this is not a story about Asia. Japanese high school girls clutch mobile phones designed by Apple in California and manufactured by a Chinese company as they head over the Hachiko crossing in search of handbags made by a nineteenth-century French brand, Louis Vuitton. It's not Asia's story because these mobile phone owning teenagers have much more in common with their foreign peers than they do with their parents. This diaspora that appears so removed from our own world, ultimately will both shape it and become it. So this is a story of the future that challenges many of the notions that seemed to hold in the pre-digital era.

61% of the world's youth sleep with their mobile phones. In my years of researching young people's mobile behavior,

I've witnessed the gamut of qualitative answers that reinforce this statistic: the phone under the pillow, the phone on the nightstand or even cuddling the handset like a teddy bear. Back in the early 2000s, parents scoffed at this behavior, but by the next decade they were doing it themselves, including the sitting-on-the-toilet-reading-the-phone first thing in the morning routine. In bed, on the toilet, on the bus, after sex. There's an app for that.

So, what drives this future? Ask a technologist and the answer will lie somewhere between 4G and 4.5G. Ask an ad agency executive and you'll be sold a big idea like "design thinking" or the term for whatever comes after "Generation Z". There are plenty of books written about these concepts, but what I want to share is the story from the eyes of the youth. Why are youth spending $400 billion a year on communication and where is it going? There are more mobile owning youth in the world than people in China. That's a significant market, but what of their individual voices? What's really happening at the grassroots level?

So why am I here in Tokyo? Progress is born of frustration. "Don't be so gloomy," said Harry Lime, the sinister anti-hero of Graham Greene's The Third Man, "in Italy for 30 years under the Borgias they had warfare, terror, murder and bloodshed, but they produced Michelangelo, Leonardo da Vinci and the Renaissance. In Switzerland they had brotherly love, they had 500 years of democracy and peace - and what did that produce? The cuckoo clock."

At the grassroots level, Tokyo appears to be anything but frustrated. The Hachiko crossing is a testament to the triumph of harmony. Despite the scale of this mass movement of people, the atmosphere is crowded, but never intense. Unlike New York, there are no mad stampedes or pedestrians enraged by a misplaced elbow. There are negligible crime, no homeless people begging for spare change and the police are conspicuous by their absence. In their place a rampant sentinel towers over the square.

Here, local food is wa-shoku with the wa standing for

anything Japanese. Although wa may have been forged by the collective needs of feudal rice farming communities, the idea runs deep into how this society organizes its urban future. When visitors first experience the modern megacities of Asia they often comment on how, despite the sheer numbers of people battling for the same resources, trains are never late and no garbage is left on the street. In place of drudgery and a life at the whims of the seasons, these cities offer pleasure and safety. There are plenty of diversions to fulfil your fantasies, from gaming arcades to stores of all descriptions. The toil of agriculture has given way to the convenience of technology: vending machines that speak to you, automatic doors in every store and mobile phones in every pocket.

So, where is the pain that drives this generation to innovate? If Japanese society is so well balanced, then why were Japanese youth buying and innovating mobile technologies back in the 1990s, perhaps 5 to 10 years ahead of their Western counterparts? By 2000, Japan and Korea had high-speed mobile internet when the rest of the world was struggling with 9kbps WAP connections. Japan's leading mobile carrier had an app store back in 1998, ten years before Apple opened its first.

To find answers we need to go beyond the shiny future we've built in the cities and see what we've left behind. In the distant rice fields where the villagers gather to earn a communal shilling by hard labor, the summer provides rich treasures for the senses: the shrill chorus of cicadas in the pine trees, the leaves rustling in the cool mountain air and the soft cackle of villagers. By contrast, young people growing up in Tokyo today know only the piped bird song that tweets from small high performance speakers on telegraph poles, the drone of female announcers wafting across the airwaves from distant mobile phone pop-up stores and the constant cries of Irrashaimase ("come in, you are welcome") from store owners. If Tokyo, a city of 30 million people, offers us a snapshot of our urban future, it's a future that is unnatural yet efficient, secure and harmonious.

However, accommodating such large numbers of people harmoniously required a trade-off. Asia had to forsake its rich communal past, replete with social infrastructure based on established relationships, for an efficient, mobile, negotiated urban future. It's this trade-off that has created the pain felt. It's a future that's largely agnostic to its geographical heritage; there are more boutiques per square kilometer than Paris, more dandy street fashions than can be found in Shoreditch in London and more ladies walking well-manicured pooches than in New York. We could be anywhere, even Seattle, from here, high up at Starbucks on my perch overlooking the Hachiko Exit.

Progress takes with one hand, while giving with the other. In the villages, rural Japanese would call out "auntie", "uncle" or "younger brother" to strangers from other towns. The old folk would stop outside the local store and pass on information about the weather, planting or neighbors. Today, however, Japan's young generation leave the comfortable bosom of their rural villages and head to the bright lights of Tokyo to live in tiny studio apartments and work 14-hour days. They find themselves lost in a sea of familiar strangers; surrounded by many people, but ultimately alone.

3 POKEBERU, TOKYO JAPAN

LESSON 1

She totters through the doorway, eyes fixed on the floor, but occasionally glancing at the rest of us sitting at the far end of the room.

"This is Ms Ryoko," says my manager, beckoning the girl towards the table.

I check my watch. Ten minutes until the end of the lesson. As my manager leaves, Ryoko takes a seat and nods respectfully without raising her gaze. She rummages in her Louis Vuitton bag and pulls out two objects. The first is an immaculate English textbook still in its plastic wrapper. The second is a small pink gadget that she clasps in her right hand. She has one eye on the pink gadget as it beeps.

"Right, shall we continue with our listening exercise?" I say.

All eyes down.

"Phone calls: Making appointments."

Ryoko stares at the pink gadget, pretends to follow the text with her mechanical pencil, then stares back at the gadget. She flashes a quick look up at me, realizes that I've been watching her all the while and sheepishly returns the gadget to her bag.

Time for conversation practice. Ryoko moves to a neighboring table with Kazu, a boyish-looking girl with short, black hair and a baggy sweater with "Oakland" emblazoned across the front. In direct contrast, Ryoko could have walked straight out of a Japanese manga cartoon: peroxide white hair and a deep tan. Whereas Kazu is 100% cosmetic free, every inch of Ryoko is somehow adorned with sparkly eye shadow, nail gels and temporary tattoos of love hearts, cute animals and teardrops. Whilst Kazu pads around the room in her comfortable sneakers, every movement Ryoko makes is accompanied by a chorus of trinkets, charms and gadgets. A small enamel panda with a high-pitched rattle hangs from one of her silver bracelets.

Less than two weeks into my stint as an English teacher in Japan, some confusion with scheduling has led to my co-worker offloading this new student on to me. It's to be expected. It's the mid-1990s and my first real career opportunity. I bought a new suit, took a flight from London to Tokyo, arrived a day early and dived straight into the Japanese work culture: stay to midnight, fill out countless forms for everything from lesson plans to attendance records and take everything that management say as gospel. I want to make a good impression and I don't want a sulky 17-year-old girl to ruin it.

"I don't like to calling," says Ryoko during the role play.

"You're a teenager, Ryoko. You love phone calls. Just pretend you like phone calls," I say, turning immediately to Mrs Yamada, a diligent housewife who likes to show off her knowledge with long, unnecessary grammar.

As we continue to practice our flashcards in pairs, I'm distracted by giggles from the other table. Ryoko's showing Kazu the pink gadget. I watch, only to be drawn back to Mrs

Yamada by her expectant silence.

"Please join our confaburation," she says.

"What?"

"Please join our confaburation."

Mrs Yamada holds an imaginary phone to her ear. I do the same.

Lesson over and I ask my Canadian co-worker, Craig, for a dictionary to search for "confabulation". As I flick through the pages, I broach the subject of Ryoko.

"Ryoko," he smiles, placing a large hairy hand the size of a bunch of bananas on my shoulder, "don't worry about Ryoko. She'll come to three lessons then disappear. If you stick to the lesson plans in the book you can't go wrong."

Craig then steers me out of his room and locks the door. I wonder what he gets up to in there. As a senior member of the teaching staff, Craig's activities go unchallenged. If he doesn't like teaching a class on a Saturday, he simply persuades the manager to transfer it to the new guy. If he has a difficult student, he renews her contract for two years and then transfers her to the new guy. Craig calls this a promotion. It's a practice frowned upon by head office as teachers rely heavily on renewal commissions and there's nothing worse than receiving a student who's all work and no reward. But Craig has clout. You'd think he was one of the first foreigners to arrive on these shores, like Samurai William. He's seen it all and knows it all; there's no culture shock he hasn't already experienced.

Craig gives me a pile of attendance sheets: the official hand-off. Next to Ryoko's name is a long line of Xs (absence), followed by sporadic Os (attendance). Craig's notes on Ryoko are unforgiving: "unmotivated", "unsettled", "distracting" are just a few of the words that leap out from 2 line appraisal. Next to Mrs Yamada's name is a clean line of

Os. In the space next to next week's lesson are the words, "past continuous". I take note of Craig's advice to stick to the lesson plan.

LESSON 2

Both Kazu and Ryoko arrive early and sit outside the class chatting in Japanese. No Mrs Yamada. Perhaps the train's delayed, I say, but trains are never late in Japan. Kazu informs me that, although Yamada has a 100% attendance record, she always arrives late, exactly 15 minutes before the end of the class.

Ryoko shows Kazu something on her pink device again.

"What's that?" I ask.

"It's a Pokeberu. Like a 'pocket bell'."

She shows me a pink pager, no bigger than a matchbox. It sits comfortably in the palm of my hand. I wave the students into the class and follow after them. The device beeps as I try to generate a response from a set of tiny keys. It looks like a fancy calculator with its number-only display.

"0...8...4...0," Ryoko says, pointing to the screen with her freshly manicured nails encrusted with gems and cute icons.

"oh-ha-yo... good morning!" Kazu and Ryoko both erupt into laughter. Ryoko hides a fierce set of metal braces on her teeth behind her hand.

I know that ohayou means "good morning" in Japanese, but I don't understand what it's got to do with the numbers.

"7...2...4." Ryoko gestures to me to type, "1...0...6."

I'm a little confused and slow to respond. I blame the stultifying humidity of the Japanese summer.

"7...na...2...ni...4...shi...1...te...0...ru...like   maru...6...no!"

she proclaims. Both girls laugh.

"Nani shiteru no? What are you doing?" Ryoko snorts.

It's the first time I've seen her enthusiastic about anything. She's no longer the vacant teenager that joined the class last week.

With only Kazu and Ryoko in the class, I let them chat away from the confines of the lesson plan. Their English grammar and vocabulary are poor, but they launch into conversation with the gusto of a child riding a bike for the first time without stabilizers. These two girls are typical of the education system: they are drilled in rigorous lesson formats, with flashcards and listening practice, but no real conversation. What they really want is a chance to express their thoughts in English.

"I dream to go to Seattle," Ryoko announces to Kazu, "but, I cannot to this." She exaggerates her disappointment with a large sigh and reaches for her pink Pokeberu beeping on the table.

Pokeberus had been aimed at Japan's middle-aged salarymen, but only 31% of them owned such a device. By contrast, 64% of high school girls had one. But not only did they own them, they developed their own language and makeshift designs to personalize the gray slab.
Pokeberus were painted bright colors and, like their owners, dressed with charms and trinkets.

This was 1995. Senior executives in the rest of the world had brick-sized mobile phones and Netscape Navigator was the cutting edge of a phenomenon evolving in Silicon Valley called the internet. When the media talked about how the "information superhighway" would transform society they also talked of the threats to girls like Ryoko. Young girls were to be protected from, not let loose in, this brave new world. In the midst of this fantasy about the "cyber" future crafted by experts and entrepreneurial geniuses, a small group of outsiders were diligently crafting the future of the world's communication industries.

When it comes to innovation, the Japanese high school girl has offered much, but has been credited with little. Take for instance, the Dengon Dial (DD) telephone messaging system launched by NTT Docomo in 1986. The official line was that DD could serve as a public message board using technology similar to voicemail. Japan had always made good use of train station noticeboards as analogue communal messaging services pre-internet, so translating that behavior to the general population should have been straightforward. In a country that continually lived under the specter of a natural disaster, a community accessed system made sense. But, by the early 1990s, it wasn't the socially minded that were adopting the service, but girls like Ryoko. They found that rather than using DD to receive public service announcements or to check up on elderly relatives, it was a useful tool for leaving messages and, in particular, dating. Thanks to a series of hacks that rapidly spread through the high school population, public service message boxes soon became ads about blood types, height, weight, food preferences, music tastes and how to get in touch.

Perhaps, like many of her elders, I've underestimated Ryoko. As I begin to think that I could learn a lot by opening my mind to new possibilities, the conversation is cut short by a knock at the door followed by a soft voice: "sorry to late."

The chatter ceases, the girls' gazes turn down to their textbooks and their shoulders sink. Mrs Yamada shuffles into the room still wearing her white gloves from cycling on her mamachari ("mama chariot"), a slow, squeaky shopper bike with a pannier at the front. She battles her way round the edge of the room, tripping over chairs and cables, with objects falling from her bag. She apologizes as she picks up each one.

Despite offering her a chair next to me, she takes a detour to the opposite end of the table. She sits, opens her textbook and looks up while clicking her mechanical pencil. I know that look. She's asking which exercises we were just practicing. But we weren't practicing.

"These girls are all about fast fashions," Craig says as he debriefs me on my lesson. "Pagers one week, some other kind of gadget the next. It's like an addiction to everything new."

"Seems a bit more important than some throwaway trend," I contest.

"They don't know what's important, Graham," Craig replies, maneuvering me towards the door. "Most of them don't even know that Michael J Fox is Canadian." He points to a large, life-sized poster of Back to the Future on his wall. "You have to understand," he says, nudging me over the threshold, "we in North America have the internet. Everything is big: big cars, big TVs, big houses, big women." He turns the lock. "We drive everywhere," he booms from the other side of the door.

I stare at the large Canadian flag adorning the closed door and hear the scraping of chairs. It must be Craig's nap time: three hours off before his next lesson. He raises his voice as he resumes his soliloquy.

"We are far more social. Whereas here in Japan they like things small. Small apartments, small cars, small families. Tiny little paper notebooks they scribble on. Even the girls are small. They don't drive as much. They take the train everywhere..."

He unlocks the door and opens it wide enough to allow a sideways glance down the hall. Assured that our manager won't disturb his rest, he re-locks the door, then concludes: "and it rains all the time."

LESSON 3

Past continuous: "I was walking to the store when I saw... X."

I need to lighten this lesson up. Why don't we try a few jokes? If Mrs Yamada is late again, we can breeze through this class off-plan.

Kazu recalls a popular Japanese joke: What are the four scariest things about Japan? Jishin, Kaminari, Kaji, Oyaji – earthquake, thunder, fire and the Old Man.

Ryoko is compelled to pick up the subject, because Oyaji doesn't just represent the red-faced, gray-suited salaryman drunkenly playing golf with his umbrella on the train platform, but Japan's wider patriarchal society.

"Nasakenai," says Ryoko, meaning "pitiful" or "beyond reproach". She shakes her head. Perhaps Ryoko's father didn't set a good example. Mr Konno embodies many of the challenges facing the older Japanese man. He regularly spends weeks away from home at a factory in the provinces, trying to sell IT equipment over a cup of sake and a karaoke rendition of "My Way". He took the job three years earlier after he was made redundant from selling Winnebagos. But it isn't this itinerant lifestyle that makes Ryoko resentful of Oyaji culture. In fact, the animosity fades the less time Mr Konno's at home. When he is at home, he whiles away most of the time in his underpants in front of the TV drinking Sapporo beer and cleaning his teeth with a small wooden toothpick. Ryoko's father is one of the 38% of Japanese men who in an Asahi newspaper survey spends less than 30 minutes a day speaking to his wife.

In the meantime, Ryoko's helicopter mother speculates over the size of her husband's annual bonus and fusses over E-coli outbreaks. On the rare occasions Ryoko is at home, her mother is at a loss to explain why her daughter spends hours lying on a futon sending messages to friends on her Pokeberu. Then there's the times when Ryoko's out all night, which is most nights. She returns in the early morning from who know's where. Just like her husband's, her daughter's life happens somewhere else and often with few tangible results.

So, like many of her generation, Ryoko's strongest loyalties lay with her peers. Rather than return to her cramped apartment, she floats with the crowd to South West Tokyo and hangs out with millions at the Hachiko crossing. From the cramped Dogenzaka roads full of love-hotels to the pokey backstreets of Shibuya, Ryoko and her friends roam in search of gaming arcades and Belgian waffles.

Many of Ryoko's mother's generation, like Mrs Yamada, struggle to comprehend. Whilst her generation was instrumental in rebuilding an economy left broken by war, these teenage girls seem to shy away from hard work. Craig calls them "parasites": a generation of layabouts living off their parents and interested in little beyond the superficial.

When we practice questions and answers in our English lesson one of the first questions asked is, "how old are you?" Mrs Yamada asks the girls, but they don't return the question. Even while learning basic English grammar, they are still aware of the subtle nuances of social positioning. For young girls like Ryoko, the social dynamic of modern Japan can be stifling. She is acutely aware of the limiting expectations placed on her as a young female, but she is given little encouragement or clear direction on how to change her situation.

In the mid-1990s the Kogyaru - the word is a corruption of ko ("young girl") and gyaru ("gal") - began to enter the mainstream media. With their bright colors, platform shoes and overt behavior, the Kogyaru were conspicuous by their bravery. During the rush hour, these girls sat on the train using cigarette lighters to warm and curl their eyelashes, seemingly oblivious to the social norms of polite society surrounding them. By comparison, their male counterparts wore dark blue slacks and button-up, chin-high collar blazers, reminiscent of traditional naval uniforms. Much of Japan's social dynamic is unspoken. So, every time a teenage girl booked a tanning session, glued the top of her loose socks to her knees or spoke in loose tones, she was sending a message.

In Japan, the words On and Giri mean everything is related. In the world of On and Giri, everything has its rightful place: either naka ("in") or soto ("out") of the group and this sense of belonging forms the basis of Japan's Wa. The naka world girls like Ryoko grew up in was one where the unmarried ones were often called "Christmas Cake" – they got stale after the 25th. The Kogyaru took one look at that world and opted out. Oyaji hegemony crafted a society of burikko girls ("high-pitched women") who bowed deferentially to their Danna-san ("masters"). The mothers of the Kogyaru sat patiently in the other room waiting to serve their masters a beer. They protected their china doll complexions from the harsh Asian sun with Chanel umbrellas. But, Ryoko's generation was the resistance. They visited tanning salons to become ganguro ("burned face"), bleached their hair the color of a yamanba ("mountain witch"), spoke with coarse masculine voices and wore garish clothes. The Kogyaru were the punks of their generation who lived very much soto the mainstream and a disruptive force in society.

Although the Kogyaru rebelled against the mainstream they weren't inverting its needs, merely its priorities. The Kogyaru still maintained close Giri-On relationship structures, just ones where Oyaji norms didn't feature. Ryoko's friends, for example, were categorized and defined. There were the Jimo-tomo from Jimoto no Tomodachi or "same neighborhood, different school", the Chu-tomo, those friends from junior high school who now attended different schools and Ona-chu, the closest group, who attended the same school.

When the world's first mobile internet service, i-mode, launched in 1998, experts foresaw a technology perfectly suited to the needs of the Oyaji: stock markets, news, mobile banking and businesses were touted as the core drivers. Within two years, however, these services found limited success; the companies that were making money were those providing games, entertainment, horoscopes and photo-messaging. The social needs of the Kogyaru were so strong that they prioritized the tools that would help them to maintain their relationships. Hence the blogs, novels, poetry, comics and shopping recommendation sites that dominated the i-mode usage chart. These were driven mainly by the Kogyaru mobile owners, not executive interests. If young girls were going to create their own narrative, they needed to control the tools used to tell the story. Rather than a tool to reinforce the existing Oyaji hegemony, technology became a powerful tool in the resistance.

Mrs Yamada finishes off her sentence with an unnecessarily long pause.

"Before..." I interject, "I've never been there... before."

Mrs Yamada nods and scribbles in her notebook.

"Time's up, I'm afraid. Next week, lesson number four. Past tense and storytelling."

The students all peruse the contents of the lesson.

"Next week, I want you all to tell an interesting story from your past."

Mrs Yamada looks nervous.

"Are you okay?" I ask.

"Difficult," she says tilting her head with the characteristic Japanese inhalation that you experience when asking a store clerk for a refund. Before I can ask if there is a problem, she's gathered her bag, gloves and books, and is out of the door.

LESSON 4

It's story time. Now the students can do most of the work. After three weeks in Tokyo I'm starting to feel the strain of deliberately enunciating nine hours a day.

We finish our "used to" flash cards and I volunteer Mrs Yamada to go first to get her story out the way, because I'm sure the girls will have something more engaging to share.

"I used to..."

She pauses for an awkward amount of time.

"I used to..."

"Go on," I encourage.

"I used to living in Canada."

"Canada?"

Ryoko, Kazu and I stare at Mrs Yamada. Visibly trembling, Mrs Yamada turns pale, then recalls her story.

Her husband went to work in IT for a Japanese company based in Toronto because he saw it as an opportunity to improve his English and get promoted. Whilst Mr Yamada did 16-hour days, including four to five hours of English language classes a week, Mrs Yamada stayed at home. She thought that Toronto was "too cold, too dangerous, too dirty, too far and too difficult." The people spoke with strange accents and drove on the right. She couldn't find a Fendi store like the one in Tokyo or sushi rice that met her expectations. After a year of trying to start a new life, Mrs Yamada persuaded her husband to return to Japan. Mr Yamada took a face-saving, unpopular assignment in remote Hokkaido where he now works for nine months of the year, leaving his wife to fend for herself down in Tokyo and keep busy with English lessons twice a week.

So engrossed in Mrs Yamada's narrative, I lose track of time. We are five minutes over.

"Erm... thanks, Mrs Yamada. That's all we have time for today."

Ryoko and Kazu sit with their mouths wide open as Mrs Yamada silently gathers her books and pencils, puts them into her straw bag then shuffles out of the room, never to be seen again.

LIFE AFTER YAMADA

After Mrs Yamada's unexpected story, I begin to hit my stride and my teaching life in Tokyo becomes more enjoyable. I rely less on Craig's insights and begin to look forward to the weekly conversations in class. The students are more settled and Ryoko even brings new English study books to the lessons.

However, as a foreigner, there is a constant stream of culture shock. The Japan 101 guide reminds you to remove your shoes, avoid pointing and not to blow your nose in public, but nobody ever gives you the social rule book. You're met with the endless civility and hospitality of your Japanese hosts, but there's an immutable boundary keeping you on the soto to the naka inner circle. To any foreigner who overcomes the initial tourist euphoria of living in Japan, the concept of being a gaijin ("outside person") is felt acutely in daily life.

Mrs Yamada becomes a distant memory until one afternoon several weeks later. As I head towards the elevator, I hear a familiar voice. Mrs Yamada swiftly exits the manager's office clutching her straw shopping bag with both hands. She is bowing furiously, repeating, "Yoroshiku onegai shimasu," a term that has no direct translation in English, but is said whenever you request something of another person, like an extended "please". Mrs Yamada reverses into the hallway, then turns towards the opening elevator and catches my eye. After an obligatory nod, she's gone. My manager calls me into the office, but the phone rings and she waves me away again.

Kazu and Ryoko sit patiently outside the class.

"Does Mrs Yamada change the class?" asks Kazu.

"Erm... I don't know, Kazu. Perhaps she has. I'll find out after the lesson if you want."

I was starting to get a little nervous that I had upset Yamada and she had just filed a complaint to the manager about this new insensitive Gaijin teacher.

"Oh, omoidashichatta!" ("that reminds me") says Ryoko. "Last week I saw Mrs Yamada in Kinokuniya (a book store). She saw to me too. Mrs Yamada says she have a trouble listening to Mr Glaham's English. Mrs Yamada doesn't understand British English well."

What was more surprising? That Ryoko and Mrs Yamada spoke to each other in public or that Mrs Yamada hadn't a clue what I was saying all along. The first is plausible: the Japanese can put on a good public face even when dealing with people that they have little time for. The second didn't make sense as neither Ryoko nor Kazu had problems. It was an often-heard excuse used by students who preferred to blame the teacher for their poor attainment. Slightly taken aback, I gesture for Ryoko to continue.

"Yes. So I say to Mrs Yamada, 'why don't you try Canadian English?' Then I show her the Canadian English book section. She was very happy."

"That's great," I say. "Maybe Craig can teach her again." We all burst into laughter, knowing that Mrs Yamada's excuse was as unlikely as Craig taking on a new student. I cut my laughter short when I notice the large figure of Craig hovering by his classroom door looking in our direction, drawn to our conversation by the liberal use of his name.

The next three months of classes are a breath of fresh air. Ryoko has a 100% attendance rate and is determined to pass her English certificate so that she can study abroad. Although she never alluded to the incident, I'm sure that Mrs Yamada's story flicked a switch. Perhaps she saw Mrs Yamada as a woman who watched an opportunity pass by with regret. Perhaps she looked at Mrs Yamada and saw an older version of herself. In time, Ryoko brings sheets of notes into class and asks me about the present perfect conditional, idioms and gerunds. As a girl with little formal education, the scarcity of options presented to her by society mean her lighthearted frolic in the world of English has become a more concerted effort to find an open door.

This weekend, Ryoko is going on a homestay to San Francisco for six weeks. It's everything she's been dreaming of, but when Kazu tells her that she won't be able to use her phone in the US she appears deflated. I reassure her that life existed before mobile phones and, besides, her host family will have a landline if she needs to contact anybody. I have a lot to learn. Ryoko says her goodbyes to Kazu and promises to bring back some omiyage ("souvenirs") and to stay away from those blonde-haired, blue-eyed American boys, although we all know curiosity will get the better of her.

In time, classroom life returns to normal with fewer incidents and less laughter. With flashcards laid out in front of me, tape player cued up for lesson 14 – "It's hot in the summer, isn't it?" – I psyche myself up to face the 9am class. Clockwork in its tardiness, a knock comes at 9:05am. An image of Mrs Yamada poking her unwelcome head around the door races through my mind. I open the door, to see my manager holding out a postcard. I stare at it. A picture of Kurt Cobain from Nirvana.

"Is this your friend?" she asks thinking that my "friend" Cobain has sent a photo of himself to me.

But before I turn it over, I see the back of Mrs Yamada's head outside Craig's room. She bows repeatedly, holding her straw shopping bag in both hands.

"Come in," Craig enthuses through a clenched smile. He turns to me and scowls.

"Sorry to late," says Mrs Yamada.

"Don't worry," booms Craig, "we'll get started straight away on the listening exercise."

They enter the room, with Craig closing the door behind them. I hear the tape rewinding and the familiar scraping of chairs. I picture Mrs Yamada sitting at the opposite end of the table to Craig, with Craig fuming internally as his three-hour coffee break is rudely interrupted. His resistance to taking on new students wasn't effective against the determined lobbying of his manager by Mrs Yamada, who was convinced that she needed an education in Canadian English. But, this is the mid-1990s and every English language school is struggling for business.

The tape recorder kicks in with the opening music to a well-worn lesson. Through the walls I hear the tinny introduction: "Lesson 2: I saw Tomoya when I was jogging."

I return to my room and settle down with The Japan Times spread across my desk. Then I remember the postcard. I turn to the back on which is scrawled, "Mr Glaham, 724106? from Ryoko."

4 BLUE MOON MULITA, VENICE BEACH USA

I'd like to say the idea for this book was born out of some high-powered business meeting. There we were, rolling up our sleeves, turning up the air conditioner as the marketing director loosened his tie and wheeled out the flip chart: "Gentlemen let's get to work."

But it wasn't. It happened here, waiting in line to buy a Blue Moon Mulita taco.

In one of those brief moments of lucidity when the noise from the adjoining bars and the clamor of beautiful people spilling onto the sidewalk gives way to silence, I turn to those standing in line behind me, chatting with excitement fueled by an energy that betrayed the late hour, part alcohol and part anticipation, and I realize what this is all about.

I'm on Abbot Kinney, an airy boulevard that runs diagonally up from Marina Del Rey and out to the old fishing village with its, now more familiar, backdrop of high rise condos, hotels and beach style homes that characterize the Pacific coast south of LA. It's a warm evening in the early summer and a throng of locals in their 20s and 30s begin to congregate in a semi-orderly line at an agreed spot on the sidewalk. Everyone is waiting. My contact in LA, Ian Votteri, brought me to this hangout just outside the crowded Brig bar at 1515 on the south end of the strip. Ian is a reliable source of what's going on in the hip and happening world of Southern California: he's spent several years helping ESPN to build up their XGames franchise, so he pretty much knows everything you need to know when it comes to youth culture, action sports and trends.

"It's on its way," he reads from the latest update on Twitter.

We start to discuss Taco options, but our volume of chatter becomes light. Our attention is drawn to the crowd. At first there are no more than half a dozen people. But, within 20 minutes we're just short of 50. A voice cries out from the back and all heads turn to see a white truck powering its way up the boulevard.

The truck pulls up parallel to the sidewalk and a South-East Asian man in chef's overalls beams out of the truck's extended catering window. He waves at a group of girls in the crowd who return his gesture; possibly regulars. Looking at the menu you can see that this is no ordinary catering truck: grass-fed organic beef, sushi-rolls, fusion tacos, kimchi quesadillas and a Vietnamese banh-mi "Nom Nom Truck" sandwich. This menu gives you an idea of how the Kogi truck has grown from a small niche offering followed by the devoted few, into a Venice Beach institution.

Kogi's success story can be told in two ways. The first, as told by the media: Mark Manguera, his wife Caroline and their Korean-born friend, chef Roy Choi, went into business serving Asian fusion food out the back of a truck. South LA County imposed tight zoning and licensing laws, so few restaurateurs were able to take the kind of risks that an operation like Kogi's could. Kogi had the scope to experiment, whereas bricks and mortar restaurants had high overheads and limited options, so had to stick with a formula that worked – Italian, Mexican or Sushi.

Nothing new here, but the story of Kogi's rise to prominence is more than the right guys being in the right place at the right time. There was Twitter and it's at this point that the story diverges: one path follows the trend, the cool use of mobile social media by LA's youth and the other leads us to social spaces and connection.

The combination of a food truck and Twitter could be an obvious social media case study. When Manguera found traditional media too slow, too restrictive or too expensive, he turned to Twitter to advertise Kogi's truck movements. When he tweeted, "Friday 12–3pm South Figuerola Street", lines began to form at 11:30. By tweeting the location and schedule he was able to build a small fan base, one customer at a time.

It's the kind of story the media loves. It titillates but never leaves us pondering the deeper questions. It has the quirkiness of innovation that fuses two seemingly unrelated concepts. It also has the reassuring subtext that this is no more than a fad and it will disappear in time: here's something novel, they tempt us, but it's not going to change our lives.

It's going to be some time before we get served.

"Couldn't we have ordered delivery?" I ask Ian.

"Then you'd miss all this." He waves in the general direction of the crowd.

This is the second version of the story. It's about what lies beneath the veneer and often escapes public attention: the story of social space and our universal drivers to connect.

To understand Kogi's success, first you need to understand why time–pressed young people value standing in line for an hour waiting for a truck to arrive. Many people have difficulty waiting for five minutes at McDonald's; they eat lunch on the fly or skip it altogether. So why were these young people willing to indulge the food truck?

If you can explain the anomaly, then you can understand

the emotional relationship between young people and technology. It's not a story about these tools, but their function in the wider narrative. Mobile phones, the coffee cup and Blue Moon Mulitas are just tools, actors in an unfolding tale about how we connect with each other.

STARBUCKS, SHIBUYA JAPAN

In Starbucks Japan, I see students reading books, housewives playing with their keitai ("mobile phones"), girls picking at their paper coffee cups and giggling as they recall last night's escapades in Roppongi. A lone schoolboy drinks a mocha.

When its CEO, Howard Schulz, first considered expansion into Japan, both the US and Japanese media were abuzz with opinions on how this American upstart coffee brand was doomed to failure. To many outsiders, Japan was a world of paradox where ceremony coexisted with technology and violent Anime cartoons with perhaps one of the lowest crime rates in the developed world. So, how could Schulz's soto Seattle brand hope to penetrate a land that had Ganguro Gyarus, Anime fetishist and a penchant for game shows featuring light torture?

The Japanese, said the analysts, preferred tea to coffee. They were generally too busy to lounge at cafes and even if they did want to drink coffee, they were already served by vast numbers of vending machines and the smokey Kissatens with their uncomfortable wooden seats. Like the Yamanote subway line at 08:30 in the morning, the Japanese cafe scene in the 1990s was already jammed full and it wasn't a particularly comfortable place for a Gaijin. Schulz, they advised, would be better off looking elsewhere.

Somewhere along the line, Schulz was underestimated. This nation of tea drinkers was remarkably at home lining up outside the iconic green font facing Shibuya station. This wasn't about content. This wasn't about products. This wasn't about coffee vs tea, US vs Japan or Starbucks vs the vending machines. This was about something more fundamental that transcended all of these arguments.

Many know that Schulz's epiphany came during a summer holiday in Italy where he saw baristas treating coffee with love and respect. In the coffee bars of Milan, coffee making was an art form, with the foamy cappuccino head as the canvas. But, to say that coffee was made is to miss the point. If you wanted coffee to be made you could always opt for McDonald's where they'd make you an inoffensive, efficient cup of coffee for 150 yen ($1.50) in less than 90 seconds. Schulz wanted to capture the spirit of coffee: the way it was roasted, dried, ground, tamped, frothed and then poured. Seeing the Italian baristas talking freely to customers taught Schulz that drinking coffee wasn't about what was in the cup, but about being part of a wider social scene; a chance to plug into the essence of society.

To say it was about the marketing of coffee is as much a distraction as saying that the success of the food trucks was about mobile or Twitter. Starbucks charged four to five times more than McDonalds. Common business logic fails to explain why young people, those with the least money, were willing to pay extra. Few know the real truth about Starbucks and Seattle. The original Starbucks store at 1912 Pike's Place just off Seattle's fish market won't immediately reveal why the formula worked in Japan, but, understand Seattle and the picture becomes clearer. Seattle is the US city with the highest rate of inbound migration, with more young Americans moving there than any other city. These large numbers of migrants mean that more young people are uprooted from their communities and left without an established base of friends. They sleep on floors, cobble together their careers and rebuild their social networks. It was no coincidence that one of the biggest sitcom successes of that era was a story about a group of misfit friends from out of town who made their coffee store their local hangout. It was also no coincidence that Schulz called Starbucks the "Third Place" – with the others being work and home. If anywhere was going to give birth to a third place it would have to be the city where people needed it the most. Could the enduring and universal appeal of Starbucks be that it isn't about coffee, there are many better coffee shops out there, but that it fulfills our most basic need: the need to connect?

Italy's barista culture grew from the Arabic traditions that migrant workers brought with them from the rural deep south when they settled in Milan and Turin after World War II. Between 1951 and 1971, nine million Italians left farming communities and found new lives in the city, each bringing with them a longing for a lost community spirit. Just as the youth of Seattle descended on cafes, the rural Italians formed communities in the north, and the young migrants of China sucked into the megacities congregated in internet cafes to chat, exchange news and sleep. The story of social space reclaimed reincarnates in its local manifestations. While each variant has its own twist and flavor, the shared truths remain the same: the life left behind was at its heart a communal one. Villagers worked and ate together. In Japan, village traditions still permeate urban interaction. You don't call strangers "man" or "woman", "he" or "she" as we do in the plain speaking, transactional West, but obasan ("auntie"), onesan ("older sister") or ojiisan ("grandfather"). In the West, calling a stranger "grandad" is almost solely used in the pejorative.

In Japan, they talk of the nabe with reverence. It's a communal clay cooking pot used for stew. Every year, as November draws close, city dwellers in their rabbit hutch apartments become nostalgic for the fresh white sheets of snow in their home towns and the nabe. For Tokyo's 30 million people, winter enforces periods of isolation and a breakdown of daily social life, but in the rural communities, the cold encourages congregation. They gather in the evenings at family homes to share stories, eat Kiritanpo made of chicken rice and burdock, and drink the local Jizake rice wine until either it or the conversation runs dry. Home towns like Fujisato, a small hamlet of just 4,500 people nestled in a well-contained valley at the base of the imposing Shirakami Mountain, underpin the social heritage of modern living. There is a solitary sushi bar, two ramen shops and the remote Subari Shinto shrine where locals pay their respects to the gods of the river, trees and earth. Unlike the relentless pace of Shibuya, the calming rhythm of Fujisato is influenced only by the order of the seasons. The lush green of spring signals time for planting rice and fruit in the orchards; the vivid orange of the fall means locals pool their efforts to harvest the crops. Life may be limited materially, but it's abundant with connection. When Japanese say "Nabe wo kakomu" ("We sit around the nabe"), it isn't an act of doing, it's a feeling.

The nabe stands for the collective goodness that bubbles up from the clay pot, shared in conversations, cooking together and having an Asahi beer or Shochu after a hard day's work. It has bound together countless Japanese, young and old, for centuries. Modernization hasn't just changed the soul of young Japan: it's as relevant to the gyaru of Shibuya as it is to rural migrants in Jakarta, young blacks in Johannesburg, middle class white kids in South London and LA, or Turks in Dusseldorf. This is the human story that manifests itself with a panoply of actors. What Starbucks teaches us is the nature of the story. People everywhere are compelled by two social drivers:

Belonging: Not only does Starbucks actively encourage people to hang out and use it as their own front room, but it also plugs into the iconic imagery of the Manhattan 20-somethings next door – Monica, Ross and Friends who just dropped in on their way home. Schultz also referred to Starbucks as "the Social Network" before pundits started using terms like "Social Media".

Significance: Not everyone can afford a $4 cup of coffee on a daily basis. In fact, Starbucks entered the market 20% above the price of a premium coffee in order to separate itself from the other cafes out there simply peddling coffee. While the bean is the mainstay of the business, it's the 720,000 permutations of beverage – from the choice of skinny, soy, decaf; to sizes, to your own choice of cream – that make it significant. There's a combination just for you and when you order a "skinny decaf latte to go" you sound just the part.

When Schulz entered Japan he made two good decisions:
1) Don't listen to the voices that say, "we're different here."
2) Change the content not the context.

His advisors recommended that Starbucks should bend its no smoking policy because every Japanese cafe allowed smoking: it was de rigueur. Yes, the Starbucks product line was different: you could find Matcha (green tea) lattes as well as Sakura (cherry blossom) frappucinos, but it was still Starbucks. The same logo, the same dark wood furniture and the same recycled brown napkins that go in the hole by the counter with the wooden spatulas and nutmeg.

A wise old marketing exec once shared with me the secret of his creative work: "Don't sell the benefit," he said, "sell the benefit of the benefit." It's not the benefit – the coffee – it's the benefit of this benefit –the social context – that really compels us to act. Young girls don't flock to Starbucks to drink coffee, but to reclaim the social connection that they have lost. If this need to reclaim wasn't universal, Starbucks Japan would have failed, but this need appears to be culturally and linguistically agnostic. Starbucks Japan is the most profitable franchise per square foot globally.

Connecting Starbucks Japan and the food truck scene in LA would be a challenge if your worldview saw only products and markets. But when you look at people and their drivers, not just who they are, but where they're from, you see two stories spun of the same yarn.

VENICE RECLAIMED

Today, Venice is a town of beachside performers, fortune-tellers, artists, jugglers and cyclists that populate the boardwalk during warmer months. Ten years ago, however, it was a no-go area riddled with drugs and gang-related crime. You would panic if you had taken a wrong turn and ended up on a beachfront, where the only people hanging around would have been crackheads or their dealers.

Today, the darker side of Venice has moved on after the authorities made a concerted effort to clean up the suburb and attract a young, hip crowd with their disposable cash and appetite for consumption. It's Venice where wild child Lindsay Lohan began her house arrest. It's Venice where young celebs like Keira Knightley and her boyfriend choose to be regularly spotted strolling along the beach. By 2010, Venice had re-established itself as one of California's coolest locations and a magnet for young professionals, designers and the freewheeling art community alike.

As with all instances of social change, the moniker of cool may be won by an upcoming neighborhood in a handful of years, but infrastructure is always slow to adjust. Tight zoning combined with rising rents meant demand for quality food in Venice fast outpaced the ability of entrepreneurial restaurateurs to provide it. Unlike the more established and less mobile communities – those that have social infrastructure, community centers, churches, family ties, regular eateries and watering holes developed over generations – young Venice residents moving into conversions just off the beach found themselves without these central hang-outs that are so pivotal in social lives.

And this is where the media so often gets the story wrong. For years, the residents of LA could have gourmet food delivered, so the quality of the product wasn't the main draw. It was this: a living, breathing community. If the restrictions imposed by real estate pricing and local authorities meant creating a social focal point would take too long, too much money and, therefore, prevent owners from taking risks, they'd have to bypass these restrictions. Parisians had their cafes. Italians had their piazzas and Londoners their pubs. Venice would now have its own community: a pop-up meeting place where locals could plug into the vibe, contemplate the world around them or just feel, for a short time at least, a sense of belonging.

EATING ALONE

FIf you want to understand what motivates us as a species, consider the objects and rituals we gather around ourselves in everyday life. As an observe, you won't go too long without observing people interact with either food, or their mobile phones. In many ways, food and mobile phones serve similar roles. Both are integral to society, both make us happy. When we celebrate, we eat and we send text messages. We don't enjoy food because it tastes good but because it feels good and as, we'll discover later this emotional connection to the mobile phone is they why question we often fail to ask.

But first, the golden arches. It's here you'll understand more about the feeling that makes food (and later mobile phones) integral to our daily lives.

At McDonald's, happiness, can be a solitary experience. The "Happy Meal" is for one. Nobody wants to be "one". Ask marketers what consumers want and they'll talk about "One-to-One" marketing. But people don't want to be singled out; they want to be helped to connect with others. When you connect them, you give them something that they can value as much as life itself. When you try to create a One-to-One conversation, they call it spam.

In the US, 80% of McDonald's lunch revenues come from drive-thrus: food eaten primarily alone in a car. The McDonald's drive-thru was first created on 24th January 1975 near Fort Huachuca army base to service the military personnel who were prevented from leaving their vehicles in uniform. What started as a necessity soon spread by word of mouth to military families and friends. In time, customers weren't only coming from the base, but from the civilian population. McDonald's found success amongst the time poor who were either too lazy to leave their vehicles or too busy to socialize around food.

Once food became less of a tool for social interaction and merely a fuel for sustenance, it could be assembled by cheap, unskilled labor forces. It's a testament to the efficiency of an organization that has $30bn worth of customer interaction annually, that it can be managed by teams of teenagers. Perhaps, what's more revealing is how we live our lives: predominantly eating alone.

It would be easy to deduce that the reason why we eat alone is that we choose to or somehow enjoy it. It "suits my schedule" and I don't have "time for long, drawn out lunches." But if you survey the online community to find out what people think about eating alone, you reveal a disconnect between the culture and our real social needs.

"...A dreaded experience."

"...An uncomfortable experience."

"Is eating alone an act of bravery?"

"Why is eating alone so difficult? (Psychology Today)"

Perhaps this explains why when we do eat alone on a daily basis, for instance, at lunchtime, we do it in the privacy of our cars, on a park bench or behind office partitions out of sight.

What marketers, restaurants and town planners easily forget is that we have all the efficiency we need. We have BlackBerries, Twitter, Facebook, online calendars and Google Maps to name a few. Nobody ever waits for a friend these days without using a mobile phone. 20 years ago, you'd wait at a bar or a station entrance not knowing if your friend was late, had forgotten or was waiting over the other side. Meetings were often a haphazard affair. We allowed every retailer "28 days for delivery". I remember sending off a check in the mail for a T-shirt for my favorite band in the 1980s, The Clash. Six weeks later the envelope returned with a hand written note stapled to the check: "I'm sorry, but that T-shirt is out of stock." Our lives adjusted accordingly. Yet with all the available connectivity today we still find ourselves craving for context: the part that cannot be made efficient and run by teenagers following a McDonald's script.

As our world becomes more efficient we grow acutely aware of a gnawing agitation that runs deep in our collective being: the need to reclaim lost relationships and social contact. In a world where we pay undue attention to the labels on the food we eat, we are, paradoxically, becoming unhealthier. The longest living societies – the Cretans, the Greeks, the Italians of the Alps, the Okinawans and the rural French – are those that eat well. "Well" isn't necessarily as nutritionists would have it. The French live longer than Americans, but eat all the "wrong" things: animal fats, dairy, wine and so on. "Well" in this sense may not be what we eat, i.e. the content, the component parts of the food, but how it's eaten. The French may be eating off the nutritionist's chart, but you don't catch them at the drive-thru, eating out of sandwich cartons or for that matter, eating alone. Look around us and we see Sunday lunch, Bar mitzvahs, weddings, Eid at the end of Ramadan, tea ceremonies and Chinese New Year, all timeless examples of how food was meant to be eaten with others. When ready-meals were first marketed in the 70s and 80s to a new generation of microwave owning middle class consumers, packets would indicate the meal "serves 2". Today, however, the packet tells you how it is. Today's ready-meal "serves 1" because we are resigned to the fact that eating alone is the norm in our busy society.

Our social heritages and collective experiences are based around the communal acts of eating. Some high-powered Parisian executives may be adopting the efficient habits of their American counterparts, but you'll still find a legacy culture across Europe that values the long lunch and eating socially. When you strip away the context from the content, you see only food labels, products and efficiency. When you appreciate the bigger picture you see how food trucks, Starbucks, nabes and other social spaces have come to exist and the crucial psychological and social roles that they play in our lives.

Kogi doesn't just represent quality fast food. Like Starbucks, it's the whole social package and it's this social package, this nabe, that offers the "collective goodness" that has been stripped out of our lives by the rampant march of McEfficiency. Nothing can replace the handwritten Christmas card, that face-to-face meeting or waving goodbye to a loved one at the airport. The more our lives are dominated by drive-thrus, whether they be literal or analogous – online social networking, online shopping, digital file sharing, virtual conference calling etc. – the higher the premium we place on the tools that help us to reclaim the social spaces stripped out of our lives by society's relentless search for efficiency.

THE MYTH OF THE DIGITAL NATIVE

Youth aren't digital natives, but offline immigrants and it's this reality that defines how they use technology. When you consider mobile usage in the US, it's Hispanics that regularly outrank other ethnic groups. But, if it was all about ethnicity, then why not African Americans? The answer lies not in who these people are, but in where they came from. Hispanics are most likely to be first generation immigrants from Latin America. They, like those that moved to Seattle and Tokyo, made a conscious decision to extract themselves from their existing social infrastructure. They are, in many respects, alone and trying to rebuild their networks with the tools that they have to hand. The mobile phone is perhaps the most powerful tool to help them reclaim what they have lost.

And that's why the story of the immigrant reclaiming and redefining lost social space is also that of the youth. Growing up has many parallels to immigration: you leave the bosom of the secure familial home with its defined roles and relationships in search of a new life. In both immigration and adolescence, people are outsiders. So they seek the tools that help them to re-establish their social significance and belonging.

Traditional research defines people by who they are: age,

gender and ethnicity. What I've found in studying youth and mobile culture is that we need to start thinking about defining people by movement and change. It's these change agents that have left their traditional socio-economic definitions behind to make a better life and it's also these change agents who drive the future of the mobile industry.

5 CIGARETTES VS MOBILES

TEEN SMOKERS

1996 number of US teens that smoke 32%
1996 number of US teens that own a mobile phone <5%

2010 number of US teens that smoke 23%
2010 number of US teens that own a mobile phone 94%

My biology teacher, Mr Potter, would stand firmly with his arms crossed and deliver his moral indictment on smoking. Perhaps it was evolution's own self-righting mechanism to shorten the lives of those who had escaped Darwin's natural selection. Somehow, the brain of a smoker was smaller, less adept. Smoking stunted the growth of young boys, made you unattractive to girls and caused cancer.

There are a lot of things about cigarettes that don't make sense to nonsmokers. And those issues were even more distant on those wasted afternoons playing truant from school: flying high on the swings in the park, out of uniform in cafes or behind the tidal break at the beach. If there was ever evidence that we, as a species, act on emotion and not logic then it must be there for all to see in the humble cigarette. Why would perfectly well-educated children – and adults – buy a product that could ultimately kill them?

With my research hat on, youth smoking has always been of interest because it's the Black Swan that indicates that our beliefs about people may not be as robust as we once thought. Young people have plenty of time to refuse before the addiction takes hold. There's a nauseating feeling that accompanies the first dozen cigarettes. There's the financial cost that acts as a significant barrier to entry. If marketing a product was about selling its strengths, then why would a young person, perfectly aware of the implications of starting a lethal habit, decide to smoke that first cigarette?

For years, governments have campaigned against the scourge of smoking by young people. Since the 1970s the young have been shown extensive videos of the tarred and diseased lungs of smokers, heard first-hand testimonies of hardened addicts breathing from airways in their necks and threatened by the punitive actions of schools and parents. Did it work? No. Teen smoking continued to rise right up until the mid–1990s.

But then something changed. Something happened in the mid–1990s in the US that stemmed the tide. Had young people suddenly come to their senses and taken heed of the weight of evidence that proved the dangers of smoking? Unlikely. Had young people suddenly started listening to their parents? No. Had cigarettes suddenly become unaffordable or unattractive? No. I was curious as to what the missing variable was: there must have been a factor that was previously unexplained in the story of youth smoking and it must also be a variable that challenged our understanding of the role tools like cigarettes play in our social interaction.

Back in 1995, I sat in a bar in London with friends from university discussing our future plans. It was the last time I would get to talk to them for a long while, as I was about to leave on a journey to Asia that would see me eventually living and working in Tokyo, Japan. Sat in a circle, we discussed careers, mortgages and relationships. As we talked I noticed how everyone had their cigarette packet neatly laid on the table, each displaying a brand and style, with or without a lighter. That scene seemed insignificant until a similar situation arose in the late 1990s. A slightly older and more weathered group of friends sat around a table in a bar and once again shared stories about the past and our hopes for the future. But rather than cigarette packets and lighters arranged on the table, there were mobile phones. Gone were Marlboro, Camel and Lucky Strike. In their place were Nokia, Motorola and Ericsson.

When I started mobileYouth these behavioral anomalies fascinated me. Back in 2000 the industry was, and still is, very much concerned with the world of content: the stuff we make. It was a world of features, technologies and fabricated concepts like "mobility", "infotainment" and "connectivity". Nowhere did people talk about real world things, like cigarettes. It wasn't only a different vertical sector, it was also very analogue and therefore uninteresting. And this was precisely the reason that I wanted to explore this area more.

I was curious. What happened if you took teen mobile ownership data and overlaid it on the previous smoking data? To my surprise a strong correlation appeared. Teen smoking grew since records began until 1996. Mobile phone ownership for late teens rose every year from its first appearance on the radar in 1996. For many, the correlation is too bizarre, too remote that it can be nothing more than chance. But, for me, this correlation made sense when you considered the context, not content of mobile phones, particularly for young people.

SOCIAL TOOLS

In a research study entitled The World Unplugged, young people from all over the world were asked to live for 24 hours without their mobile phones. As a condition of the study they had to remove the batteries from their devices and share their feelings 24 hours later. For some young people, the absence was bearable, although uncomfortable. One boy reported holding and playing with the phone in his hand, despite it being dead, simply to "feel reassured". Another shared the common feeling of nervousness. As the data came in, a clearer picture of the youth mobile relationship emerged:

"I feel trapped. I don't know what's going on in the world," reported one high school student from Brazil.

"I felt lonely without multimedia. I arrived at the conclusion that media is a great companion," said a student from Chile.

"Five hours in and my typically relaxed Sunday has had the adverse effect. Raised heart rate, increased anxiety. I'm panicking not knowing what is going on in not just the outside world but also my world. My friends, my family, my life," reported one teenager from the UK. "All I wanted to do was pick up my phone and become a part of the human race again."

"I feel dead," shared another student from India.

"I felt like a helpless man on a deserted island in a big ocean," reported Eric, aged 17, from Indonesia.

Eric's plight was shared by many and without respect for borders. Michelle, aged 18, from the UK reported, "not knowing what to do with myself." She constantly flitted back and forth between the bedroom and the kitchen. At first, she distracted herself by grazing on morsels of food. Then she rifled through the letter drawer under the microwave in search of something to distract her from the gnawing pain of loss.

Piece by piece a picture emerged of a whole generation irritated, directionless and lost. How could this have happened?

For 17-year-old Eric in Indonesia, the prospect of life

without a mobile phone and the internet was the stuff of nightmares. Eric's mobile phone was his oxygen. He slept with it every night: read BlackBerry Messenger (BBM) before placing it on his nightstand and falling asleep. It was there first thing in the morning, recharged and ready to deliver his morning update of news and gossip.

It's easy to see the world as ruined by technology and seditious marketers, like Billie Joe Armstrong from Green Day said. It would be a world where the stories of Xiao Zheng were "just waiting to happen". We are too quick to dismiss the research findings with common one-liners like, "We didn't have mobile phones when we were kids and it didn't do us any harm." But we fail to see what lies beneath the content of the story.

When we were kids, we played out until dark, we sat in the cockpit as we flew out on summer vacation, we knew phone numbers by heart and some even had archery lessons at school. Teachers didn't see any harm in children eating peanut butter sandwiches and they didn't have to close the school because the path was covered with snow. Children took the bus home, smoked on the way and talked to old men who weren't pedophiles. Sure, the dark recesses of humanity have always existed, but we've allowed the media to cajole us into making our children fragile and fearful, which led ultimately, to a Chinese boy selling his kidney for an iPad2.

Children today can't play without their parents structuring it for them. What exactly is a "play date" and whatever happened to our children simply playing with a ball out in the street? When young people grow up in a sanitized world where all the inefficiencies of chance are squeezed out of their interactions like a templated McDonald's production line then we are left with a generation that lacks the robustness to interact.

HACHIKO

Standing watchful over the four million people leaving

Shibuya station's busiest exit is a low-key bronze statue of an Akita dog. His name is Hachiko, after which the exit is named. Hachiko's legend began in post-war Japan where the hound would accompany his master every day on his way to work and wait faithfully until the return journey home. Even after his master's death, Hachiko waited patiently at the same spot, day in, day out, until his own death 12 years later. The story is etched onto the consciousness of modern Japan. Perhaps Japanese youth today empathize with this unconditional loyalty.

It could be the comfort of family members, loved partners or even a pet. We all have experienced this chemistry, but what exactly is it? In a recent psychology experiment, scientists measured the levels of oxytocin, a chemical produced by our brains when under stress, in young girls when communicating with their mothers. They found that when girls contacted their mothers remotely by BBM oxytocin levels remained stable. However, when the girl and her mother were in the same room, oxytocin levels fell dramatically. Mobile phones can never replace human contact and young people today do not see mobiles as the preferred alternative. Mobile phones are a proxy: a tool that helps to maintain, not to improve our social interactions. In short, what they really want is offline, real world contact.

So when we consider the story of Xiao Zheng and his kidney, it doesn't seem so crazy after all because it's a story written in the hardwiring of our brains. Sure, if we write the story off like my biology teacher, Mr Potter, Zheng is just a materialistic spoilt brat who should have known better. But understand the motives and the backstory, and a different narrative emerges. Here's a young boy who grew up as an only child, removed from his rural community and transplanted to the city by his family. He lived in an apartment without any social space to play, explore and make mistakes. As a nation, China is reaping the economic and social benefits of the mass migration of its workers from the rural villages to the East Coast. People like Zheng's father, an itinerant factory worker who lives up north, build the parts that help to fulfill the world's need for cheap plasma TVs and refrigerators. As with all applications of efficiency, somebody has to pay the price. American youth grow fat because we insist on cheap, industrial food and China's youth grow isolated because we insist on cheap electronic goods. Zheng only sees his father during Chinese New Year: a hectic week spent eating and exchanging presents to make up for lost time. We still don't know the impact of this migration on an estimated 200 million people. It's often described as the biggest migration in history, but it's not about the past, it's happening right now.

For the most part, this young Chinese boy has little of the social infrastructure his parent's generation had. He lives under the constant specter of failure should he not score straight As in his university entrance exams. The western media bangs the drum for more testing to help us catch up with the Chinese, but the discoveries of the greats, like Newton and Einstein, weren't born in textbooks and science tests, but in their ability to think creatively and it's this fundamental ability that's being stripped out of young people's lives. Innovation is born of play. Zheng feels isolated, and insignificant. Against this backdrop, it's easier to understand why someone may see sacrificing a kidney as better than a social "death". When we understand the "why", things don't look so stupid after all.

Our social behavior is hardwired into our brain. The idea of "digital natives" is a myth because it's this social need and not digital technology that defines youth today. Ready meals for one, traveling by car and the quest for efficiency are breeding a disconnected generation of youth deprived of the contact and infrastructure that previous generations once took for granted.

6 LONG ISLAND, USA

Danielle's mom thinks Tommy Jordan did the right thing, although the jury is out on his use of a handgun. In the confines of the family's Oldsmobile, Danielle is compelled to listen to the parental verdict as she gazes vacantly out of the window.

In September 2011, Tommy Jordan achieved internet notoriety when he posted an eight-minute video on YouTube excoriating his 15-year-old daughter, Hannah, for posting malicious comments about their family on Facebook. In the video, he criticized Hannah for her lack of gratitude, values and respect, exacerbated by the fact that her inflammatory comments had been posted using a notebook PC bought for her by Mr Jordan. Whilst many viewers weren't shocked by the content of Mr Jordan's rant, what happened next was stunning in its unpredictability. At the seven-minute mark, Jordan pulled out a .45 revolver and fired two rounds into Hannah's computer. Case closed.

"He was just laying down the law, honey," says Danielle's mother, as the car ambles its way up Long Island. "He was setting an example. Okay, he was a little excessive, but, in spirit, you can't fault him."

Danielle looks up and sees her mother reflected in the vanity mirror of the passenger seat.

"He's a jerk," mumbles Danielle, as her mother continues.

"She lives under his roof and she has to accept his rules."

Danielle stays quiet, rolls her eyes and sighs her frustration both at her mom's strong views and the cramped conditions of the car. She spends most of the next hour fighting with her younger sister while her parents engage in some conversation about the history of the Island and the endless achievements of her classmates, reported through the lens of their parents' middle-class bragging. Danielle occasionally feigns interest by responding with a "yes" or "I know" as she checks her mobile phone for a signal, a message, a status update, something that connects her to where she wants to be.

One more hour to go before they reach the campsite. The mobile signal wanes. Danielle stares at her phone. Zero bars.

"For God's sake!" she says.

"Honey, I told you about using that language, didn't I?" says her mother.

"We told you about using that language, Danielle," her father says demonstrating his habit of adding little to the argument except an echo.

"A week? I can't survive a whole week without my cell phone," Danielle cries.

Her dad interjects: "You'll survive, just like last time."

Last time? Her dad means last summer, when she didn't have a mobile phone. She didn't have a phone because her parents had seized it. She spent a whole week at home feeling isolated, not knowing what her friends were doing, not having the constant reassurance of messages and status updates that kept her in the loop.

"I almost died," Danielle says.

Her father shakes his head. As is typical of teenage hyperbole, she suffered, but she didn't exhibit any fatal symptoms. For Danielle, however, a week without her phone was social death.

Last summer, aged only 15, Danielle's behavior started to push the boundaries of acceptability laid down by her parents. One day she took the train uptown to the Apple store whilst on a date with a friend of a friend from high school. When her mother found out, the household erupted with of the noise of slammed doors and feet stamping up the stairs.

"No, you don't have a boyfriend," shouted Danielle's mother, who concluded the argument by confiscating the phone.

As the parent of any teenager soon learns, children are more industrious than they're given credit for. Sure, they struggle to find the motivation to do their math homework, but set them the challenge of how to send text messages without a phone and they throw themselves into it wholeheartedly. Before long, Danielle discovered an app for her iPod that enabled her to send SMS. When her parents thought she was diligently studying and listening to music, she was really lying on her bed with her iPod plugged into the socket, sending up to 100 messages an hour to a small group of friends.

There were a lot of other things Danielle's parents weren't aware of. For example, her relationship with Alex (Danielle didn't want to share his real name for fear of alerting his parents who were as strict as hers.) When they met at Molly's summer party, Alex promised Danielle that he'd get in touch. He didn't ask for her phone number; instead he checked out Molly's profile on Facebook, found Danielle and sent a friend request. Within minutes Danielle had picked up the request on her mobile phone, responded and the conversation had begun. As active adults we'd assume a conversation about shared interests, weekends, families and so on, but that didn't happen until much later in their relationship. At the beginning it was more a case of Danielle posting ambiguous lyrics to a song on her Facebook wall, which Alex would "like". He'd then ask her questions about what they meant. The conversation would switch to a flurry of text messages on the phone. Was she angry? Did he say something wrong?

"Creeping" Facebook became a key method for measuring the health of their relationship, with both Danielle and Alex regularly checking each other's walls to see what was going on. When Alex accepted a friend request from another girl, questions would ensue. When Danielle's friend posted an inflammatory wall update that was picked up by a friend of Alex, the drama would begin.

When she was alone at home or her sister was in another room, Danielle would switch on the PC, fire up ooVoo and start a video chat with Alex. Sometimes their chats would last for four or five hours with bursts of conversation interspersed with long periods of silence. This wasn't chat as adults know it: sometimes Danielle would be reading a book and Alex playing on his Xbox, both at different ends of Long Island, with the video humming quietly in the background. Sometimes other friends would join in, creating a network of four or five interconnected rooms all simply hanging out and doing little of obvious merit, as teens have done since they first got their own bedrooms.

To say their social video chat was pointless undermines the effort that Danielle and Alex invested in getting in right. She would take great care in crafting the right lighting conditions and would strategically place photos of friends in the background. He would choose the right baseball cap, wear it just so and co-ordinate the rest of his outfit to make the right impression. To the outsider, these nuances of communication are easy to miss or even to dismiss as worthless, but it's these nuances that create value in the medium itself. 90% of communication is passive, but because we observe youth in unnatural conditions – focus groups, market research communities or online – we miss out on these subtle social expressions.

When technologists think of teenagers using their products, they're easily seduced by creative agencies into believing the active myth. In advertising, teens are seen on skateboards, high–fiving each other or broadcasting a "look at me" video from a concert. These scenarios do exist, but they occupy a small proportion of teen life. The inconvenient truth of how young people interact with technology is that it's very passive and, in many respects, mundane. Mundane it may be, but unimportant it isn't.

Observing how young people use technology is a lot like watching gorillas in the zoo. You go to the zoo expecting the gorilla to do something interesting. Why doesn't he run up to the bars and rattle the cage? Why doesn't he beat his chest and bare his teeth? In reality, the gorilla, like the teenager, does a lot of what appears to be nothing. Gorillas sit around picking imaginary ticks out of each other's manes as a grooming task; a process that seems rather pointless, but has an important role in reinforcing peer group relationships.

When Danielle and Alex were communicating via video for five hours, they weren't doing it the way the industry wanted them to. They weren't goofing around at concerts or rocking out to Lady Gaga as cool teens in the adverts did, but simply lounging around doing what teens do best: annoying their parents by appearing inactive. When they watched the same movie, there were four screens involved: two televisions and two computer monitors. This is too messy for most technologists to contemplate in their orderly world where everything converges on one device.

Danielle and Alex's summer romance was made possible by modern technology, but it was distinctly traditional in its origins. In essence, it resembled the innocent, early steps in the relationship between Danielle's parents, Diane and Bill, who, just like her, grew up on the Eastern seaboard of the United States. Back then, they didn't have mobile phones, so teenagers had to go to where they knew others would be: diners, milk bars or other public hangouts. It's there that Danielle's parents met, in a milk bar in New Jersey where Diane worked. On their first date, Bill drove Diane down to the beach where they walked across the sand dunes for hours. The milk bar has long gone and, today the beach is all but closed off to the public; walled in by private access walkways and a conveniently constructed tidal break that serves to keep both the waters and unwanted visitors out. Many other public spaces are now controlled with "no loitering" signs and monitored with CCTV. When Danielle wants to go out, she has to plead with her mother to drive across the county or she goes to structured school activities such as volleyball and, much to her dislike, clarinet lessons.

For Danielle, her mobile phone is a lifeline, the space her parents do not control. It's where classmates creep each other's pages or click the "like" button in a modern equivalent of the hangout. The trading of these non-verbal, passive social signals transcends the understanding of the logical, active adult. It's this logical lens through which we view youth behavior that renders it meaningless to us.

To industry pundits, teens are fleeing Facebook: they are conspicuous by their absence of activity. But once you look below the surface you begin to see another picture. Teens aren't fleeing Facebook, they're just not using it the same way that we active adults would do. Rather than post updates – "I just boarded a plane" – teens are creeping each other's profiles, communicating passively, just like the gorillas grooming each other. The other side to the story is that teens aren't fleeing Facebook; they're avoiding adults and marketers. Danielle's bedroom door has a large "Keep Out" sign on it, demarcating her private territory. Similarly, teenagers are actively shutting out unwanted guests on Facebook.

Parental infiltration is inevitable. Teen social space is under attack. Danielle would conceal her phone at high school, often making excuses so that she could head to the bathroom to check her messages. Since the phone ban at school, teachers reported a marked increase in stomach cramps, menstrual issues and weak bladders. One classmate's anger with school officials for confiscating his mobile phone resulted in a childish tirade where he said he would, "blow up the office where the items were kept under lock and key." He soon felt the full force of his off-hand comment. Police raided the school, arrested the pupil and whisked him off to be charged. He has since been excluded from school. His crime? Being a frustrated teenager.

Danielle couldn't refuse her mom's friend request, could she? And what about the teachers and older cousins? Eventually, Facebook became less like the bedroom space she was painstakingly stage-managing and more like a functional kitchen where everyone gathered.

Teenagers, however, adapt. When her older peers headed down south for Spring Break, they were acutely aware of how their antics would be recorded and posted on Facebook for boyfriends, parents and future employers to see. Many toned down their behavior. Danielle's industriousness in finding an alternative to texting on her mobile phone illustrated an energy and drive that wouldn't easily be contained by concerns about how the outside world would react. Many young people have already adapted their messaging habits and use Facebook for creeping friend profiles, SMS or BBM for gossip with close friends and boyfriends and social video for hanging out.

The fear of being starved of social contact drives teenagers to innovate ways to stay connected and that continues to create a dynamic tension between parents and children. We see teenagers hanging out doing little – outside the 7-Eleven, in their rooms, in parks – and we feel like they're wasting their lives. But we forget that we spent an inordinate amount of time hanging out, watching TV together and creating our own social spaces.

"I didn't survive, Dad," says Danielle, placing extra emphasis on the word "Dad" as if he had willfully neglected his responsibility as the family protector.

Danielle's dad looks into the rear view mirror and sees his daughter staring at her lifeless mobile phone. To him, the absence of the phone is a good thing. The security and safety of his daughter is what he wants to ensure – but at what cost?

7 RIYADH, SAUDI ARABIA

"I can remember it clearly," recalled Ahmed as he scratched his beard.

"The blacked-out family SUV had just speeded up the driveway to our house, with my mother half hanging out of the rear door, shouting, 'Where are they? Where are they?' She was wailing, 'Do they have a gun? Where is your brother, Fahad?' She was gesturing for us to run towards the safety of the car's open door."

Ahmed's tone turned reflective as he stared into the bottom of his beer glass. He laughed half-heartedly.

"We were just kids, playing. We didn't think about the consequences. We just wanted to see what it was like outside. Play in the garden like you see in the movies. My poor mother. I always disappointed her."

Ahmed's words echo in my head as I'm driven along the road piercing the desert landscape. Along this desolate conduit heading out of Jeddah airport, the asphalt carries few people, only dust. There are vast monuments to ill-spent wealth: from unoccupied office buildings to empty superhighways. There are no statues or paintings to grace the public spaces. A mobile phone advertisement emblazoned across a public billboard offers a tantalizing promise of connectivity beyond the confines of Saudi Arabia's stultifying protocol.

Green lanterns fill the night sky: the minarets of distant mosques. Everyone exists at a distance. When you do catch people close by, it's a group of Bangladeshi immigrant workers venturing into the scorching desert heat to break rocks for the new highway or a group of women hidden under their black abayas and niqabs – the full body tent and veil that orthodox Muslim women wear in public – being ushered into a large chauffeur-driven people carrier. A security guard holds open the car door and surveys the environment as if shielding a celebrity caught by the paparazzi while shopping in Hollywood.

The world Ahmed invited me to – that of Saudi Arabia's privileged elite – is one that happens behind closed doors. They live in the air-conditioned confines of their huge homes, behind large steel security gates. The children, trapped in a similar A/C bubble, play Call of Duty on the PlayStation, hunting down a team of Arab terrorists before turning occasionally to one of their two BlackBerries to message a friend. Beyond the family, the little contact most Saudis have with the outside world is with an underclass of immigrants drafted into this ghost economy to build roads and care for the sick. They share their lives with Filipinos maids, South Asian servants and cousins. Many are taught by private tutors, rather than attending school. It's understandable how in such a world, where contact beyond the tightly controlled family unit is limited, outsiders are viewed with distrust. When the teenage Ahmed and his younger brother, Fahad, decided to venture out of their comfortable family compound that fateful afternoon because they were curious about what it would be like to take a walk, their returning mother caught them on the road and wrongly assumed the worst: that kidnappers had raided the property.

I stare at my Yemeni driver from the back of the car. He speaks little English apart from "Brown?" He was the only person who came to greet me at the airport. He held a card with my name printed in bold letters, and transported me out of the make believe world of date palms and indoor waterfalls into this barren void. He shouts something in Arabic as we speed off down the highway towards my reunion with Ahmed. He gestures violently, dismissing imaginary flies.

"Brown? Not brown!" he says turning towards me and pointing at the pale jet-lagged face staring back at him, urging him to keep his eyes on the road. He releases an insane laugh over his shoulder and reveals a set of rotting black teeth surrounded by cracked lips and gray stubble. I wonder if this is what Ahmed meant when he generously promised that, "My family will see that you are well looked after," when we first met in Dubai last spring. It was his offer that lured me here and has me sitting with this half-crazed Yemeni driver whizzing through a cloud of dust as he continues to jabber to me over his shoulder.

My reason for traveling to Jeddah is a tenuous one: a chance meeting in a bar in the Emirates while watching a Chelsea soccer game. Perhaps after a beer, my judgment was dulled and curiosity got the better of me. At times I wonder why I got involved in this unfolding narrative, but Ahmed's family is bankrolling the visit. And they pay well.

Business in Saudi Arabia, like a familial relationship, values unswerving loyalty and acceptance over accountability. So when Ahmed invited me to help him secure funding for his mobile phone related franchise from his shrewd uncle, his family paid for my visit based on Ahmed's word alone. But as my driver pulls up to the family hotel, I'm beginning to wonder what Ahmed is really up to. Here, everything is inshallah, mashallah, bukrah and malesh ("If God wills", "by the grace of God", "tomorrow" and "don't worry about it/it's okay.") Business is less about being competitive and more about understanding how things work – or, perhaps, how to work people. Take many of the public works, for example.

Money regularly disappears as it filters down from the rich oil sheikhs and through many hands. Ahmed's family had to wait five years for a sealed road to be built to one of their hotels because the project kept getting shelved or stalled due to corruption that is rife in the system. By the coast, where Jeddah meets the Red Sea, a desalination plant produces prized drinking water. The precious water is then made available in the public square through an imposing fountain before being jetted back into the sea. Why such conspicuous waste? There is one explanation: anything can be done because if no one probes your personal affairs, then you won't ask any questions about theirs.

Back in Dubai, Ahmed was open as he sat in the hotel bar with a relaxed, almost regal pose, bare foot up on a stool. Oblivious to the obvious social taboo of a Muslim drinking alcohol, he fanned his face, reddened due to a few too many beers. He was an old head on young shoulders, speaking in manly tones from deep inside his portly frame, his words accompanied by slow, premeditated gestures. His looks betrayed his 20-something years. The tufty beard growing around his chin made him look as though he'd just started shaving. Beside him an improbably tall and pale Finnish man, Jarko, shouted in harsh, staccato tones, flailing his gangly arms at the grass-colored screen. Our common interest in the soccer game led to a conversation about business. Ahmed told me he was there on a reconnaissance trip.

"I need to find some new suppliers, raise some more capital," he explained while chewing on a large handful of cashews. I can't spend all my time shopping here." He pointed to a stuffed Gucci bag sitting under the bar stool containing at least three ribboned shoe boxes. Women's shoes. Ahmed said he wasn't married, so I assumed they were for his girlfriend.

"Ja ja," chimed in Jarko, "we want to bring in phones which open up a new world of apps to Saudi youth."

"Like games?" I asked naively.

"No no... dating," replied Ahmed, his friend nodded enthusiastically. "That's what it's all about. And you Mr Graham?" he asked.

Saudi youth own, on average, 2.5 mobile phones each. The average high-school girl owns 3. So, Saudi Arabia has a voracious appetite for the latest mobile phones, as well as the fashion for blinged-up Versace or Dior cases. But, Ahmed was trying to cater for a growing market: youth who wanted specific apps.

I explained that I had been researching young people and mobile phones since the 1990s and had made a business out of selling this research to mobile companies. He listened attentively and nodded approvingly while cracking open monkey nuts. Based on a rather brief summary of 15 years of work, Ahmed had convinced himself that I was the missing link for his business. I was foreign. I was white. So I was an "expert". Now all Ahmed had to do was convince me to come to Saudi Arabia to look credible in front of his rich uncle and his deal would be finalized.

When pushed on the subject of his business plan, Ahmed seemed to know little detail. It's not that he didn't understand the market need: Saudi Arabia had a pent up demand for dating services. He was just more preoccupied with privacy than the market. His talk veered back and forth with Jarko on how they could encrypt messages, delete pictures and cover their tracks. All of this was required because of market "inefficiencies".

"What do you mean, 'inefficiencies'?" I asked.

"Muttawa," he replied, "Religious police."

Ahmed went on to deliver the Muttawa 101, a list that pretty much consisted of lots of "don'ts". Don't head through customs in Riyadh airport with a laptop bag on display. It's easy pickings for the muttawa. They'll stop and more or less strip search you, checking your gear, not for drugs or alcohol, but technology prohibited in the Kingdom. Don't even think about bringing videos in on your computer. Don't take photos in public, especially not near to the muttawa. The list went on.

Referring to the muttawa as the "secret" police is a misnomer as they are both conspicuous and everywhere. But young Saudis carry themselves with a confident swagger that both accepts the omnipotence of the muttawa and somehow dismisses them as nothing more than the bogeyman: the muttawa exist, but they won't catch me doing anything (as long as you adhere to the 101).

In many ways, Saudi society prides itself on that swagger, even to the point of misguided confidence. Ahmed sold me on the idea of staying at his family's five-star state of the art hotel, but on arrival it appears to be in some kind of 1980s time warp. Lebanese and Filipino staff continually sweep dust from under formica chairs that decorate the foyer. Everyone is busy looking busy: shuffling papers on the check-in counter or attentively watching the glass doors, waiting for a coach party that never comes. The hotel is probably hemorrhaging money like all those other projects in the desert, but as long as nobody asks, nobody seems to care.

I'm led to my room where a message sits on the bureau. It's from Ahmed. He wants to meet at 9pm in the hotel restaurant. Just enough time to freshen up and maybe five minutes of shut-eye. The bathroom taps aren't working, so I call reception. Five minutes later a thin, dark skinned South Indian man dressed in a brown uniform enters the room and makes straight for the faucet. He shakes his head from side to side and says something in his local language, Malayalam, before the pipes begin to cough and sputter forth a brown liquid. He takes out his mobile phone and shouts something at full volume to the person at the end of the line. He then points to his watch as if to gesture this will take time and promptly leaves.

Just after 9pm, Ahmed greets me with all the confidence of

a sheikh, aristocrat or relation to the Crown Prince, which he is not. He's dressed in his white thobe (traditional dress), red and white head scarf and black sash belt.

"This is my Uncle Rizwan," he says introducing me to a larger version of himself who hovers over the table, breathing heavily, with sweat breaking on his brow from the short walk from the other side of the restaurant. Rizwan wears a simple white head headscarf: a sign of his authority.

We sit on formica chairs as a waiter promptly attends our table, offering bowls of water and hot tea. I look up to see the South Indian man who "fixed" my bathroom plumbing earlier. He nods in acknowledgement and utters the words, "some drinking?"

Back in the Kingdom, Ahmed's mood is different. Gone is the relaxed, carefree opportunist I first met in Dubai, and in his place is a hard-nosed businessman with all the formalities and social graces that would be expected from someone in the presence of his conservative uncle. Ahmed launches into a long monologue about mobile phones and young people. He grabs my laptop and points at a series of hockey stick shaped graphs juxtaposed with Saudi Arabian flags. Flicking back and forth between the data he liberally drops English words into his Arabic speech like "scalability", "word of mouth" and "communications revolution". His uncle listens, occasionally opening one eye to glance at the computer screen. At the end of the pitch, Rizwan nods, gruffly mumbles something in Arabic, then leaves.

At first, I think he's gone to the bathroom, but Ahmed's reaction signals that our five-minute meeting was a success. He gazes after his uncle, confirming that he has left the premises. Then the weight of convention lifts from Ahmed's gait. His rigidity gives way to a more youthful stance.

"Come, I take you to hookah!" he says, ushering me swiftly to the exit where his driver waits. He turns and reads the uneasy expression on my face.

"Hookah! Smoking bubbly!"

"Oh...I thought you meant..."

Ahmed bursts into laughter, shaking his head dismissively. It's the first laugh I've heard from a Saudi since my arrival. I don't smoke, but I'm relieved nonetheless.

We're driven into the town center in the back of Ahmed family's S-Class Mercedes. He's within easy earshot of the uniformed driver, but Ahmed seems to care little of what his servant hears, sometimes treating him like he doesn't exist.

"You see, here in the Kingdom," Ahmed explains as he stares out at the harsh, dry landscape, "it is difficult to meet the right girl. When I was a young man," the 20-year-old Ahmed continues; all talk of business has evaporated, but not the swagger, "we used to drive into town and follow girls. But we could never talk to them. In America or The Great Britain, it's okay. Here, it's not allowed."

Ahmed's tells me about the beneficiary of his shopping trips to Dubai: his girlfriend. But he uses "girlfriend" in the loosest sense of the word. You see, Ahmed's never met his "princess".

"I saw her once from a distance. She was entering the shopping mall with her cousins. I knew it was her because she had a rhinestone-studded shoulder bag and Gucci sunglasses," he says.

I picture four girls entering the doors of a shopping mall: a pretty girl with a shoulder bag wearing dark glasses turns her head knowingly to Ahmed and smiles from a distance before disappearing into the crowd. But, I soon realize that couldn't have happened. The mystery quartet would have been hidden under their black abayas. His girlfriend's face would have been covered by a dark mesh over which her Gucci sunglasses would have been placed. If it wasn't for her sunglasses and handbag, she would have been as indistinguishable as the rest of them.

"Did she see you?" I ask.

"No, she has never. I cannot send her a photo because if she gets caught with my picture she is in trouble."

"How did you...," I struggle to find the appropriate word to describe their virtual encounter, "... meet?"

Ahmed "met" his girlfriend through a Bluetooth-enabled phone. Then they agreed to move the conversation to the riskier text messaging. Unlike Bluetooth, text would leave a trace on the network, but the risk was worthy of the reward. Without knowing where she lived or any details about her family, Ahmed managed to build a reasonably impressive profile of her life: what she liked doing, where she hung out and what sites she visited online. They hadn't talked about her plans for marriage yet, because Ahmed had avoided broaching the subject lest his bubble burst.

"She's just normal Saudi girl," Ahmed says. "Very beautiful."

He's never seen her face. Ahmed recalls with excitement her adventures: small triumphs in life that tell of a girl trying her hardest to escape an oppressive environment. Once she asked her driver to take her and her friends into the desert where she removed her abaya and drove like a maniac around the sand dunes. Saudi women aren't allowed to drive. Her desert sojourns became a regular occurrence until her family Range Rover Sport became stuck in a sinkhole and they had to call out her brother to rescue them.

After several weeks of text messages, the communication broke off and the girl disappeared. Her father had confiscated her phone following the incident in the desert. Ahmed only found out two weeks later when she managed to get back online via an app installed on her iPod. They've been in regular communication for nearly five months and he still doesn't know her real name. He only has the postal address of an office where one of her cousins works, to which he is planning to mail the shoes. To Ahmed, she is simply known by her Bluetooth handle "Prisoner of Tears" – who likes Gucci shoes.

"I cannot marry her," he says.

"Don't you like this girl?" I reply.

"I can't," is his only answer, the conversation drops into silence as he glares out of the window. His confident gait retreats into a resigned slump.

I use the silence to reflect on our conversation. I can only guess that he can't marry her because of his parents. As a young Saudi his insatiable curiosity and drive to explore the world was the root of a fractious relationship with his parents. Back in Dubai, Ahmed told me about the false alarm at the house and how he upset his mother that day. He also told me about a seemingly innocuous incident at the local grocery store.

"When I was just teenager my mother took us to the local Carrefour, where foreigners come for shopping. Many live up in the Aramco compound. I see them looking at the vegetables and often think, 'I want to talk to them some day'. So one day, when my mother is looking something else, I walk up to a tall blonde American man and say 'Hi, I am Ahmed. How do you do? Do you know if this movie (he gestures as if pointing to an imaginary tape or DVD in his hand) have Arabic subtitles?'"

When his mother caught him talking to a foreigner, she confiscated his television for a week.

Although he's progressed from buying $20 DVDs to $5000 reports, the motive is still the same. Starved of experience, Ahmed, like many of his generation, still struggles to find outlets for social contact. In the hookah cafe at the local shopping mall, a crowd of boisterous males gathers drinking tea and coffee, while watching Premier League soccer. But wherever Saudis gather so do the muttawa. Ahmed gestures loosely in the direction of a pair of men sitting at the opposite end of the mall keeping a close eye on proceedings. They are conspicuous by their lack of the black band (igal) around their plain white head scarves. From what I've heard, they'll stand with their swagger sticks ready for an opportunity to stamp out the fires of sin that have gripped the nation's youth using the threat of public excoriation and physical violence. Ironically, muttawa don't have the power to arrest, but they do mete out physical beatings of both men and women for breaking Saudi Arabia's strict Wahhabi form of Shariah law. And, much of these beatings are issued for incidents that involve men trying to interact with women.

"They are just criminals. Most of them are freed from jail because they signed an agreement to become muttawa. If they stop you, the first thing is they check your phone. All the evidence is there."

From my research I found that most were indeed ex-cons paid a paltry 3,000 Riyals ($100 a month) to stay out of trouble. Ahmed doesn't talk in depth about the muttawa, but acknowledges their presence as a nuisance. He simply shakes his head in a resigned manner accepting his fate: this orthodoxy is here to stay.

The muttawa's religious zeal treats any new innovation with suspicion. In the 1990s, muttawa patrols would shoot out satellite dishes on private property from the back of blacked out GMC suburban vans. Now, however, Saudi youth have access to more empowering tools, like the internet and the mobile phone. Whereas the satellite dish was a conspicuous sign of access to seditious media, the mobile phone is discrete. The phone offers access to unparalleled opportunities for dating. It's upped the ante with the muttawa, who now have taken it upon themselves to break into Saudi homes, confiscate mobile phones and beat the occupants for messaging their friends. Although their activities are not sanctioned by law, their behavior remains unchallenged.

In 1997, it was the muttawa that sponsored an edict from the Saudi king that fathers, husbands and guardians were responsible for their daughters, wives and sisters wearing the black abaya in public. If a woman was caught outside "undressed", both she and the male guardian would be beaten. In 2008, they banned the sale of cats and dogs because they were "conducive to flirting."

Women's magazines are censored. There are no movie theatres, no concert halls and no dating. Photos on public billboards and hoardings, except those of the king, have their eyes blurred. One well-known academic was caught having an affair with a student. He received eight months in prison and eight lashes. The student, being the unmarried of the two, received only four months, but 350 lashes. Their affair was well disguised until, in a momentarily lapse of concentration, the student left her phone at her sister's house.

Saudi youth are well aware of the risks of discovery, but remain unperturbed. It's part bravado and part having the right tools to remain undiscovered. In this joyless, unyielding desert, the nation's youth play a constant cat-and-mouse game with the religious police to circumvent the rules that they impose.

Technology is a powerful tool to bypass control. In the shadow of a date palm tree in the local shopping mall, Ahmed starts to show me exactly how local Saudi boys flirt with girls right under the noses of the muttawa. A man leans onto our table shouting, "I love Manchester United. My friend in Manchester. You from Manchester?" His sweaty, smiling face is pressed up against mine, his arm draped over my shoulder. Ahmed gestures for the man to sit as if swatting a fly. He then switches on his phone and discretely shows me a list of messages appearing on the screen via the Bluetooth channel. Most are in Arabic, but I can work out the tone from the cute pictures that accompany them: flowers, pink teddy bears, hearts and birds are popular. My attention is drawn to the occasional English word jumping out from the script: "Princess", "Delight" and the unexpectedly brazen, "Gay Saudi Lover." Being young in Saudi Arabia is a challenge. Being gay is punishable by death.

"This is how we do in Saudi," explains Ahmed handing me the phone as I become conscious of a distant figure standing at the far corner of the mall watching us.

"But now, not so popular. We prefer BBM (BlackBerry Messenger). We have a PC in the house, but nothing is safe. So, we Saudis use Bluetooth or BBM. See...?" he points to some Arabic script, with the motif of a horse and stars surrounding the message, "Here is a poem. I send this poem to a girl. If she likes it, she accepts my request."

He sends out dozens of poems, often the same with a slight tweak in the title, to lists of girls who advertise their availability and interest from the female segregated level of the mall below. Most will simply refuse his advances. Sometimes, if he's lucky, a girl will engage him in conversation. He estimates that less than 0.5% of his messages will get to a voice conversation. Less than 0.5%? What kind of numbers is Ahmed dealing with here?

Dating for many young Saudis has always been more scatter-gun than targeted, and Ahmed is considered, by his own modest benchmark, to be something of a pick up artist. I imagine that he pictures himself as a rich Sheikh lying casually on his luxury yacht charming Bond girls. Then he shares with me the methods he employed before Bluetooth and the imagery vanishes in disappointment. He recalls with nostalgia the days when boys would simply dial random phone numbers late into the night in the hope that a young girl would pick up. As a 16 year old, he'd sit in his bedroom punching through countless permutations of dial codes using his father's spare mobile phone, until his father saw the phone bill. He turns and says something in Arabic to his sweaty Manchester United companion who then roars with laughter. A round of manly pats on the back ensue before Ahmed turns to me and says, "I was just asking him if he remembers the time we tried to enter the women's mall downstairs. We were just teenagers. One time he is successful because he says he is a cousin. But we always get thrown out."

Ahmed tried random approaches in the street, which are illegal. It's not uncommon for young Saudi males to throw balls of paper or notes through an open car window or at the feet of a passing stranger. The girl would unravel the paper to find a phone number, email address or BBM PIN. Ahmed even resorted to throwing mobile phones at girls in public, which he tried a couple of times while his cousin was driving. They'd slow down as they passed the mall and toss the handset at a girl, with it often breaking at her feet or hitting her by accident. He admits that this approach wasn't very effective.

Some of his friends have moved on to writing BBM PINs on pieces of paper and then slapping them on moving car windscreens, but it's an approach Ahmed is yet to try. He recalls an incident where a friend was caught by the muttawa with a stack of business cards each printed with his BBM number, accompanied by love hearts and a stallion.

"Are we still being watched?" I ask.

"Always watched," he replies as he flicks through a contact list on his phone nonchalantly.

Fortunately, like many of the older generation most muttawa are uninformed when it comes to technology. But that doesn't mean that young Saudis are off the hook. The muttawa often assume that the mobile phone is the root of most amoral activity. The policy of confiscating phones, beating suspects and asking questions later is the standard modus operandi when dealing with unruly youth. The higher echelons of society, however, are more tuned in to what Saudi youth are doing. The government banned BlackBerry from operating their BBM service because it operated a closed loop, beyond the scrutiny of the religious zealots. The scenes of the London Riots and the Arab Spring of 2011 were enough for the Saudi authorities to be vindicated in their beliefs that these messaging systems are detrimental to the moral fabric of society. IP based messaging is also restricted meaning any internet messaging or communication system – Skype, MSN, Facebook messenger and so on – is closely monitored to avoid unrestricted interaction.

There is talk of the government asking manufacturers to disable the Bluetooth function on their handsets to control these youthful encounters, but Ahmed already has the answer: identify a job lot of unlocked devices and import them to his Saudi friends.

"If they stop Bluetooth," he philosophizes, "we'll find another way."
"iPhone4 has FaceTime, isn't it? Then we'll ship the handsets with Jailbreak. They are preinstalled with a patch so it can run on the 3G network. This," he says, pointing to the iPhone in his palm, "is how we meet friends. It is my well. It is like a fountain in the desert. It can never run dry. They can never turn it off."

He then switches to more urgent matters.

"I hear Harrods in London is a great store. Many of my cousins have been there. Princess is going to London. Next time, you are going to invite me to London, right, Mr Brown?" he turns and stares at me.

I was wondering when I would be obliged to return the hospitality.I feel like I'm being drawn into another of Ahmed's convoluted plans and, as a guest of his family, I'm powerless to resist.

"Maybe arrange a conference or a supplier meeting? I'll ask Uncle Rizwan for funds. All we need is an invitation."

8 LANCASTER COUNTY, USA

Danny appears contemplative, philosophical even. Optimism underpins his youthful naiveté.

"I guess this is where I belong," he says.

The car pulls up slowly on a dirt track that leads to an isolated farmhouse. Danny stays sitting in the back and stares blankly at his mobile phone screen. There's no conversation: no kind words, no emotional farewells. The only sound is the rattle of the car's rusty engine. Danny takes a deep breath and looks out across the field towards the house. A figure emerges from the front door: a woman dressed in traditional clothes and a headdress. Danny turns and meets the eye of his friend staring into the rear view mirror.

"What are you waiting for?" shouts his friend.

Without turning his head, he hears the sound of Danny leaving the car, heaving his travel sack onto the verge and slamming the door shut. When he looks around, Danny is gone.

The night before, young Danny and his friends sat on the porch of their bachelor cabin, 20 minutes ride out of town, staring into the sunset, smoking cigarettes and drinking bottles of cheap beer. Danny knew his short adventure was coming to a close. His curiosity had been satiated and he was ready to return. But, he still harbored a small desire for change.

"My uncle could use it for business at the timber yard. Once he gets one, they'll all get one. Their kids all have them anyway. Seems pointless trying to stop something that is obviously good for the community. The elders will try and get in the way, for sure, but this time it's different. They will change."

He slung his empty beer bottle into the shadows and cradled his mobile phone in his hand.

"I'm taking mine back," he said. "What can they do?"

Danny's community is the Amish of Lancaster County. This is the same community from where he's taken a sabbatical - rumspringa as they call it - to experience life on the outside. Rumspringa is a core rite of passage for Amish teenagers. At 16, they're actively encouraged to turn their back on the traditional ways of Amish life: values that uphold the community, like service and a general suspicion of technology. Amish teenagers flee farms and hole up in bachelor (and bachelorette) pads outside of town; drink beer, indulge in all kinds of wild behavior that would be seen as unacceptable in their stricter, former life. It's a process endorsed by the elders as some form of cathartic therapy for those years of suppressed teenage angst. Once they've finished their rumspringa, the young adults have to make the ultimate choice: to return to their communities and commit to its laws or to go "English", that is, to live on the outside and be ostracized by their family and Amish friends forever.

It was almost a year ago that Danny set out on his journey of self-discovery. The first I saw of him was a lone silhouette emerging hesitantly from behind a hawthorn tree into the path of our car's dipped headlights. The air was warm and thick with the dust of threshed oats and the aroma of nearby farms. Christian, our mutual contact, leant out of the passenger window and beckoned him forward.

A nervous smile broke on Danny's face, lit by the bright display of his mobile phone in the twilight. Few words were exchanged as this tall, somewhat awkward 17 year old in his clunky cap-toe leather boots, bundled himself into the rear seat of the car, sinking below the window line, clutching his black duffel bag.

I turned and smiled politely at our new passenger, but Danny just stared out of the corner of his eye, lean faced and pale. I noted that his hands were red, sore and swollen, and his clothes were covered in sawdust. He turned to look out of the rear window as we drove down the country road, the small group of farmhouses from where Danny had come, disappearing out of view. Danny reached into his duffel bag and pulled out a husk of brown bread wrapped in a small towel. He chewed frantically as if he hadn't eaten for days.

Ten minutes drive from Smoketown Airport lies a small settlement called Paradise: 60 miles from Pennsylvania and a stone's throw from the lesser-known Dutch Wonderland Amusement Park. You wouldn't know Paradise was there unless you were one of the Amish locals or the increasing number of tourists who come to gawp at a lifestyle that seems at odds with our efficient, technology driven world.

The drive out of Paradise is rich with the aroma of Amish industry: diesel fuel, sawdust, wheat and the rich harvested earth that yields everything from tobacco to potatoes. On the surface, little seems different from the rural existence of many Mid-Western towns, except that the Amish have chosen a life freed of a dependence on technology. Amish are forbidden to own cars, computers, televisions and, until recently, mobile phones.

I had no idea what to expect when I met Danny. I had little contact with the Amish save through my fixer who was well acquainted with the rebel community of the Amish that broke free to live in the wider realms of Pennsylvania. All I knew was that Danny was spreading his wings. How would he survive? Would his new life be better than the stultifying existence that shunned both outside contact and the trappings of the modern world? But youth can adapt, often faster than adults. You only have to observe how youth negotiate foreign environments to confirm that: a schoolchild can master a new host country language in two years whereas an adult takes a lifetime to learn, if at all. See how some adults would rather starve to death than look stupid ordering a food they don't know in a foreign land. Seeing Danny slumped in the back of the sedan staring into the bright, white void of his phone, it was difficult to distinguish him from any other 17-year-old American, except that maybe he was a little thinner than most and had a distinct Pennsylvania Dutch accent.

In a series of interviews conducted with Amish teens over a period of 18 months, I discovered a number of truths about what it meant to be Amish. But these paled by comparison to those truths about what it meant to be human – a social animal. Once out of their coarse, functional, handmade clothing, Amish teens started to behave just like any other American teenager. Sure, they needed to be shown how to change the channel on the television and how to use a shower, but in time, they were drinking beer, getting wasted and hitting on girls.

The most obvious differences were in how they used technology. The Amish relationship with technology has always been misunderstood and misinterpreted. Nowhere does it say that the Amish are forbidden to use technology or to innovate. In many cases, they can be highly innovative. Smallholders, like Danny's cousins, turned to high-yield crops like ginseng over potatoes, and factory owners developed diesel-powered rigs for their machinery. It was a characteristic visible in Danny's bachelor pad, where a combination of hacks and fixes kept the ramshackle cabin in a livable condition. When the supplier cut the electricity because of a late payment, Danny and his friends commandeered a small diesel engine and ran their lights from that. Most non–Amish 17 year olds would be freaking out if a simple fuse blew on their Playstation.

The Amish don't forbid technology – they forbid a reliance on technology. Needless to say, "reliance" is a subjective term, so while one sect of the Amish believe that cars are liberating, key to mobility and vital to business, another shuns them altogether, citing their capacity to break up communities once held together in a tight geographical nucleus. Without cars, Amish life is bound by a rich social fabric in identifiable hubs, mainly the home and the church. Even within sects, the phone has become a moot point. Some Amish have phones, some don't. So, of technology, the elders ask, "Does it bring us together or draw us apart? Does it promote reliance?" In most cases, they rule new innovations as precipitating isolation.

When Danny's datt and mam moved into their farmhouse, they tore out the telephone, central heating and electricity. Whereas the more liberal families were leaving the smallholdings for life in the suburbs, Danny's were pursuing a life more closely allied with the Ordnung: the Amish doctrine. The Amish still used some technology to survive and to manage their crops. Danny's datt would cut the grass with an old push mower that was, "noise and hassle free". It was quiet all right, but required real manual strength and had a habit of breaking down. Danny's first taste of mechanical engineering came when he spent one summer taking apart and reassembling that old mower with nothing but a screwdriver and a hammer.

Late night discussions at Danny's bachelor cabin would often broach subjects beyond girls, drugs and partying. The group of Amish boys would discuss the merits of life on the "English" outside in comparison to what they had left behind. Each object from the television to the extractor fan and their mobile phones would receive due attention: did it actually make life better?

When Danny grew nostalgic, he would often lament the social fabric he felt absent from his new life. Sure, he had a mobile phone to call any friend, any time, but his friends were already here, often sitting around the living room, with the television blaring MTV Jackass, staring at their mobile phone screens texting somebody else, who knows where.

The family Danny had left behind would regularly entertain unannounced visitors at their farmhouse (they had no phone): visitors such as Daniel, an itinerant Amish preacher who traveled throughout Pennsylvania giving away bushels of peaches. The guest would be treated to a meal of potatoes, beets and onions followed by 20 minutes of light chat.

"You're welcome to stay longer," Danny's mam would say, but Daniel would simply rise from the table, exchange pleasantries with Danny's datt and leave.

"Nobody seems to drop in here. You always have to schedule something," said Danny when feeling frustrated by his growing sense of isolation. "You can't go to their house and say 'hi' because they're busy doing something or they're not even at home."

Visitors interrupting our meal times are endured at best, and considered a nuisance at worst. We want a message in advance. In the Amish community, however, the people are the message. They carry news of the outside world. Families welcomed preacher Daniel not because he was a preacher – that simply reassured them that he was legitimate – but because his brief, but informative, visits were the pre-Facebook equivalent of a whole community's status update. All the while, five children sat at the table and ate with Daniel and the rest of the family. No one used a mobile phone; no one stared at a television screen in the distance; no one rushed their dinner to finish off the game they were playing on their iPad. When the meal was over, the girls would help Mam to clear the table and the boys would sit and talk to the guest. Nobody retreated to the privacy of a bedroom.

Danny wasn't the only one in his family who dreamt of greener grass. Of the five children, his estranged sister, 18-year-old Lina, went to live at her aunt's house in a more liberal Amish community. She spent her time planting celery sticks, listening to music, drinking beer and flip-flopping between remaining outside of Paradise and returning to the family nest. She sent infrequent texts to Danny to moan about life and her aunt. She urged Danny to, "Pray for me. I need a better life." These text messages contained an implicit warning to her younger brother that he'd regret not having more ambitious dreams than just leaving the community. If anything, Lina hoped that her younger brother would finally break from the stultifying controls of Amish life and realize himself in the big city.

Their brother Eli was a constant reference point; a reminder to Danny of what regret really meant. Although I never met Eli, Danny's narrative recalled a dour man of only 22 years old. As a boy, Eli dreamt of life on the open road. He wasn't particularly ambitious or inspirational, but when Danny and Eli hunted together on the farm as children, Eli engaged his younger sibling with stories of how he would grow up to be a truck driver and drive a juggernaut to California. Eli used to watch juggernauts ply the highway just outside of town and would fantasize about their exotic destinations. Eli's dreams were soon crushed after an accident at his uncle's sawmill, which left him with a walking stick and a permanent limp that provided a lifelong excuse as to why life had passed him by.

Danny and Lina used to tease their older brother, saying he was just like one of their Old Order relatives: an ongoing joke that often ended with Eli throwing a tool to the floor and kicking a door in protest before storming off to seethe in private. The relatives of which they spoke were rarely mentioned in family circles; they were too dogmatic even for Danny's datt and mam. Danny never quite knew what happened to them. But he remembered their cold milk soup, their dark and humorless household and the story of how they took off one day on a Greyhound bus heading north with a promise to start over again. The family wasn't missed, except for the two youngest children who were closest in age to Danny and Lina. It was these children's habits of smoking, drinking and "bed courtship" that riled their parents and led them to abandon the colony for a more disciplined community.

Caleb, the youngest male, was close to Danny. They would often play out in the fields while their parents discussed community news on the front porch. One day, in the hut that Caleb's uncle used to store farm equipment, Danny was shown a pair of rollerblades. He had never seen such a device: a pair of boots with wheels! Caleb was given them by an older cousin who had returned from rumspringa and needed to stash them away from his authoritarian father, who was also a village leader. Caleb and Danny would rollerblade on the rough, wooden kitchen floorboards, the only flat surface in Paradise, while their fathers were out in the fields and their mothers turned a blind eye. Often they'd blade with just one boot each, or one would take on both boots and try a trick that would always end in failure.

When Danny learned that there were more such objects on the "outside" his curiosity was piqued. He sourced a skateboard, made locally from a flat plank of plywood. He learned about MTV. He got hold of a mobile phone. The whole Amish order seemed at odds with his natural curiosity, so he came to the conclusion that the only way to live happily was to abandon the order at the earliest opportunity.

Midway through his first year of rumspringa, Danny felt confident that his tenure in the outside world would last. He found casual work at a construction site and started to consider moving on from his bachelor cabin. Maybe he could convince Eli and Lina to leave the Amish and make a better life on the outside?

"Everything's changing. I'm seeing new stuff everyday," Danny remarked with all the enthusiasm of a new arrival to foreign shores before the novelty wears off and the daily grind and culture shock take hold. In time, even the optimistic Danny, began to harbor doubts. He found himself cursing not being able to charge his phone because they had run out of electricity again. He cursed only being able to get a signal at the front of the cabin facing the car park. He began to rile at the barrage of insults he'd receive from local hicks.

"Where did you park your horse, bro?"

"Are you married to your cousin?"

He always kept his head down, even if it was just a trip to Walmart or the 7-Eleven.

Some of the Amish boys in the cabin had already succumbed to the harsher realities of life in the outside world. One of the older boys, Alex, who had spent more than two years on rumspringa, had found himself in trouble with the law for selling marijuana to local college students. Back in Paradise, his father was a senior clergyman, and here, on the outside, he found it hard to fit in and find work. Alex became increasingly obsessed with the old world and embarked on a personal crusade against the Amish community, spying on farmhouses; burning hay-bales and horse buggies. Danny and Alex would often come to blows in the kitchen over trivial matters such as the washing up, the payment of bills or simply where the car had been parked. These arguments were just symptoms of Danny's gradual disillusionment with what life on the outside had to offer.

Danny's journey back to Paradise, a year after his departure was accompanied by few words. He stared constantly at his mobile phone screen, texting friends back in the bachelor pad as well as the sister he hadn't seen for nearly 18 months. He knew that he was making a tough choice by returning to the fold. No drink, no cigarettes, no partying, no swearing, no buttons on his clothes and so on.

No Facebook? Amish still living in the community weren't supposed to use Facebook, but many teens had profiles under false names: dressed in baseball caps and wraparound shades. Some had even hooked up with Danny in his bachelor cabin at weekends, changing into their "English" clothes and getting drunk or high in parking lots before returning in the early hours beneath the radar of their parents. When you come from a family of 10 or more children, as many Amish do, it's easy for an absence to go unnoticed.

For the Amish community to continue welcoming preacher Daniel's updates, they don't need to stop the rapid adoption of mobile phones and Facebook. Many elders see developments like Facebook and mobile phones in the same light as previous fads like rollerblades: something that will eventually pass. So it isn't the untethered behavior of teens like Danny that has the Amish concerned for the future. What worries the Amish are zoning plans for a new Walmart fives miles outside Paradise. Many of the older orders claim they'll leave if it's built.

Before he returned to his community, I asked Danny if he'd give up his mobile phone. His answer caught me by surprise.

"I'd give up this yes..." He paused. "Only because it's a Nokia. I wanted to get the new iPhone4 but I can't buy it unlocked. I'm going to get it sent out to me when it comes down in price."

"How will you do that?" I asked.

"Ebay?" He looked at me as though I'd asked a stupid question.

9 VOZ DA COMUNIDADE, BRAZIL

Rene Silva dos Santos has become a household name. In 2012, he was one of four youngsters handpicked by Coca Cola to carry the Olympic torch in Liverpool, UK; 10,000 kilometers from his hometown in Rio de Janeiro, Brazil. Following his 300-meter torch relay along the city's docklands, 18-year-old Rene spoke to a local newspaper about his thoughts on Liverpool and his life back home.

"Do you like the Beatles?" asked the reporter.

"Not much," said Rene. "I prefer Brazilian funk. I have All My Loving on my phone though and I'd like to find out more about them during my time here."

Rene went on to wax philosophical about his positive vision of the future.

For Rene, life had been transformed radically. Two years earlier he was still distributing a handful of photocopied newspapers in the favela where he was born, one of more than 600 slums in Rio de Janeiro that houses up to a third of its population. Rene's world was one that both enticed and assaulted the senses: from the waft of smoky black beans steaming through a window, to the smell of open sewers and animal carcasses left to decompose in the puddled alleyways. He was well-known in his small favela circles, but outside of this world he was just one of Rio's 10 million poor who eked out an existence under the shadow of the outstretched arms of Cristo Redentor, the statue that graces the Corcorado hills and embraces the city.

Every Christmas, Rene would collect donations from local businesses, who knew him as the teenager who wrote a newspaper, and buy expensive chocolate eggs for the favelados, the street kids. Now, Rene is the recipient of multiple awards: the coveted Shorty Award, Twitter's nearest equivalent to an Oscar for social media; the Faz Diferenca ("making a difference") award from the Globo newspaper and a journalism scholarship from the esteemed Estácio de Sá University.

How Rene got thrust into the world's media spotlight was part chance, part determination and part technology. It's a story that highlights the injustices that face the favelados in their daily lives, but also gives hope through the exposure of their story to the outside world.

For many of Rio's affluent middle classes that live in the asfaltos, the formal city uptown, the lives of the favelados might as well be in another country. And like foreign issues they would have remained if it wasn't for a gradual change in Brazil's social conscience, combined with growing numbers of young people accessing the mobile phones that placed the lives of Rene and other favelados squarely on the agenda of Brazil's powerful media.

The media inhabit their own world. Less than 30 minutes from the slum in which Rene grew up are the picture postcard scenes of Ipanema and Copacabana. On those sun-drenched beaches, the beautiful people of Brazil's brash, confident middle classes - media executives, investment bankers and advertising account managers - play volleyball and football in blissful ignorance of the scenes unfolding on the other side of the city. Local merchants are only concerned with winning the patronage of tourists in white linen who saunter down the long boulevard buying trinkets or sipping caipirinhas and looking out on to the South Atlantic Ocean.

In the Cidade Maravilhosa or "The Marvellous City" that is Rio, chauffeurs ferry children to elite private schools in blacked out SUVs that stop for no man and no traffic signal. According to a security company in Rio, carjacking is a growing crime and unless you have the necessary $500 thousand to $3 million to pay the ransom, you need to invest in a suitably armored vehicle and a driver. What the driver earns in six months is equivalent to just one month of a child's school fees. These kids are the lucky ones: the ones from the asfalto that ride the wave of President Lula's economic miracle. Their families keep maids; they vacation in Europe and North America and speak with the strong American accent of international schooling. A stone's throw away, on a small rise of hills, lies the Morro where people like Rene's parents work three jobs as drivers, maids and janitors or factory workers just to put food on the table. For their children growing up in an environment where bus jacking is a growing menace, the only security they can rely on is good fortune and turning a blind eye.

For young favelados, living in the Morro means learning to survive and the first rule of the favela is never talk about the favela. You soon learn to respect the lei do silenco that binds fearful residents. On each corner a boca de fumo ("mouth of smoke") swarms with gangbangers, moleques ("street urchins"), mulheres da vida ("prostitutes") and malandros ("petty thieves" or glue sniffers yet to be subsumed into gang culture). Rio life is full of incident, as described in the words of Francis Hime's song Sinfonia do Rio de Janeiro: "Paradise is here, hell is here, madness is here, passion is here." The street has many eyes. But you never admit to seeing anything.

A sign on a disused brick wall reads, "CV, Énós" ("We are the Commando Vermelho ("Red Command")." The CV is a vicious gang that controls the area, terrorizing rival gangs, police and their own people. But, these aren't the ostentatious drug barons of Colombia, but petty criminals with automatic weapons. A young dealer in the CV can, at most, aspire to owning a car or a plasma television if he reaches the position of gang leader. Many perish in the process. Driven by desperation, young male favelados are sucked into a lifestyle that seems as condemned as the environment from whence it came. In Rio, when bodies are found in shop doorways, the backseat of cars or piled high in an open mass grave, they are usually local males aged between 14 and 25. There are around 5,000 reported murders every year; about the same as in the US, but Rio has only six million people compared with 300 million in the US. So, you're 50 times more likely to be murdered in Rio, and if you're young and male the figures are even higher. The most common cause of death for young male favelados is being in the wrong place at the wrong time.

Eulogized on YouTube with baile-style hip hop that celebrates their kills and women, the CV wage misery in their community. But they also bring their own form of law and order. Thieves are disciplined, even shot. An abusive husband who beats his wife is severely punished without trial. The CV also offers protection against rival gangs. When Rene was just 10 years old, the Morro was invaded by the ADA (Amigos dos Amigos), a gang that terrified residents and meted out random punishments, including "microwaving", where victims were entombed in tires and doused with gasoline before being burned alive. Life in the Morro can be cheap. Any form of protection, even from gangsters, is a welcome comfort.

When Rene started his newspaper at school it was to document his class projects. But when he complained about the cleanliness of the bathrooms, officials quickly addressed the problem. Rene had tapped into a medium that could create change and so the Voz Da Comunidade ("voice of the community") was born. However, there was only so much material that he could cover on the school itself. So, as his confidence grew the amateur newspaperman turned his attention to life in the Morro.

Rene wanted to write an alternative account of life in the slums. Under the influence of the mainstream media, most outsiders viewed the affairs of the favelas as being as relevant as the distant squabbles of their Argentinean neighbors or the plight of native Amazonians. For the few middle class kids who ever ventured there, the favelas were just a place to score marijuana or crack cocaine. The Morro was strangled by the unyielding grasp of poverty and terrified by gang warfare. But inside the dark hole of desperation, a glimmer of hope. It was a world where in the midst of chaos, normality triumphed. You see, there are always those who want to improve their lives. Most slum dwellers work. Most of their children go to school. Most of them want a life without gangs and, given the right platform, they want to change their circumstances.

Rene wrote about life in between the community's pockets of green and the rocky outcrops where parents would lounge on their rooftops in hammocks attached to half-finished walls as their young children rode tricycles close to the perilous drop to the street below. He wrote about the favela's rich and chaotic daily pageant: everything from the canopy of wires running stolen electricity to the red and blue Ethernet cables hanging ominously low into the street. He wrote about the mundane: one of his more successful early headlines read, "Cano estoura na rua sexta-feira" ("a very large pipe burst on the street").

For the favelados, life in the Morro was about survival despite the odds. People like Rene's neighbor, Jorge aged 24, a self-certified electrician. Although he had been interested in radios at school he obtained no formal qualifications, but he knew enough to approach the makeshift junction boxes hanging from the sides of buildings or on street signs that contained a spider's web of wires. With his rubber-handled blade, he'd peel away the plastic coating to run a new wire to a neighbor's house to supply her new refrigerator. Thanks to Jorge, student Maria was able to power her ice-vending business and serve refreshments in the morning to everyone from commuters to groups of men carrying cement on their backs. This cement could have been to build a new level for a house, to repair a broken wall or to fill a pothole. Around Maria, young males would dig up the sidewalk with makeshift tools to access an underground water pipe and run a new feed to their area.

If this game of survival was played long enough using whatever means were available to stay afloat, fate would provide a chance to escape. And so, on 25th November 2010, Rene's day came.

"Helicopter flying over. Just heard shots from Vila Grota." Rene managed to squeeze out the tweet despite the battery on his iPhone running precariously low.

It was approaching 7am and already it was the hottest day of the year. Rio was waking up to a war zone. Camera crews from local stations, carrying expensive equipment, laptops and microphones, tried in vain to position their reporters, dressed in full body armor with private security entourages. They all breathed a sigh of relief as they were turned away from the police roadblocks. They were safe in the knowledge that they had been spared the impending shootout between government forces and heavily armed drugs gangs in one of the world's most dangerous slums. Despite being rendered impotent, the journalists were fascinated by the only eyes and ears on the scene: three teenagers, Rene Silva dos Santos aged 17, Igor Santos aged 15 and Jackson Alves aged 13. In the spirit of innovation fostered in the favelados, the three were armed only with what they carried in their pockets that morning on the way to school – their mobile phones – and their only protection was a wood-framed bed and a wafer thin mattress. Concerns for their safety grew.

"Children get out of the street," a voice echoed from the loudspeaker below, "there's going to be a shootout."

Women snatched their children from under broken palettes and piles of rubble, screaming as they ran for safety behind closed doors or disappeared into a labyrinth of rat-runs and shadowy dirt streets. The burnt-out shell of a municipal bus stretched horizontally across the street, billowing thick black smoke. Before the shell strike at 7:03 am, the bus had carried school children, factory workers and laborers. Police armed with FAL assault rifles inspected the bus for anyone unable to evacuate, but no one was found. They signaled for the support team to advance and slowly, a cautious line of caveirão emerged, the first blaring out an intimidating message: "We have come to take your souls."

Caveirões were the Rio police force's latest addition to an extensive arsenal used to fight the city's uncontrollable gang problem. What began life as a security van for transporting documents and bullion soon became co-opted as a military-style assault vehicle, much like the armored personnel carriers favored by the United Nations and seen in news reports from war zones, equipped with a 360-degree turret and heavy rifle mounts. Inside, 12 heavily armed officers of the BOPE, Brazil's own special forces trained in the jungles of Haiti, carried grenades and assault firearms.

"I confirm! Intense gunfire inside Complexo do Alemão. The caveirão are heading up to Morro do Adeus," tweeted one of the boys.

His friend added, "The invasion has begun."

"We will show with exclusives direct to you live from the community! Wait a moment!" the teenagers tweeted.

Who were these boys and how did they get exclusive access to the hottest news item of the week? No, make that the decade. Mainstream media was abuzz with speculation. Perhaps they were foolhardy kids trying to hog the limelight. Perhaps they were faking it and not really in the action, but uptown in a middle class suburb.

"At the moment, 4 police helicopters flying overhead."

"I just heard 3 shots."

"The shots do not stop."

And then, the twitter feed went silent.

Brazil was changing. A new-found economic boom had been combined with the status of being an impending host to two of the world's largest sporting and media events: the World Cup and the Olympic Games. This sharpened middle class sensitivities to the country's world image. Dealing with the favelas was no longer a "foreign" issue, but was squarely in the realm of domestic policy. Faced with the prospect of foreign journalists probing the country's injustices and inequalities, politicians were compelled to act. Helped by a little funding from the event sponsor, Coca Cola, the government engaged in a clean-up program that sought to go beyond the typical commando-style raids that too often retreated, leaving communities open to the "blow-back" of gang reprisals and revenge.

When government forces embarked on sporadic eradication programs, often tied to an election campaign as a nod to the middle classes, they did so with the rhetoric of a country at war: these weren't dawn raids of drug dealer hideouts by narcotics squads, but full-on invasions by troops, armored vehicles and heavy firearms. War justified the collateral damage. An 11-year-old girl was shot by police assault teams as she sat in her home playing on the family computer. In any other situation in any other country the media would have been outraged. But this was a country where mothers regularly organized silent protest marches, holding up pictures of their loved ones caught in the cross fire, and the marches didn't even make the newspapers the next day.

On the morning of 25th November 2010, a posse composed of the army, BOPE special forces and the navy stormed the Complexo do Alemão with the objective of resting strategic points from the iron grip of the CV and the ADA. This was an unprecedented level of military activity being played out to an unprepared media: the educated, middle class graduates from the asfalto. In the early hours, the media blackout to prevent informants from tipping off gangs meant that the most significant event in Brazilian domestic policy for a decade was taking place once again in obscurity.

And that would have been the case if it hadn't been for those three teenagers holed up under the bed in Morro do Adeus using their mobile phones: an iPhone, a battered Nokia and a Samsung, to provide a much needed conduit of news from the frontline to uptown Rio and on to the rest of the world. From their first tweet announcing the arrival of the militia to 180 followers, word spread. In the absence of any credible news sources, scrambling journalists quickly followed these three teenagers on Twitter to stay on top of the action.

"What are you doing in Complexo do Alemão?" asked one bemused and slightly irked tweeter, who sensed that the dominance of the media attention for the boys was overshadowing the real story of the raids.

"We live here," replied Rene.

When news got out that the boys were nothing but young favelados in the right place at the right time, media fascination grew. By the evening, they had 20,000 followers. At the peak, their messages were being retweeted 300 times a second. As Rene set up a video stream from his phone to show the events to the world on Twitcam, his cohorts fielded questions from the media, worried friends, residents, celebrities and the blogosphere. Their followers tweeted support and messages of concern:

"I couldn't sleep, I was too nervous thinking of your situation."

"Be careful, you shouldn't give out your location. The gangs have Twitter and internet too."

"You shouldn't use your real names. Perhaps use a fake

name?"

But it was too late. The three boys were already internet celebrities and their "hideout" was easily identifiable from earlier descriptions of their location. In time, their lifelines to the outside world could only be used sparingly to conserve battery life as the community's power lines flip-flopped throughout the night. Rene would power up the phone, rush out a burst of tweets and then power down until the next update.

24 hours of tweets later, the mainstream media arrived. Small groups of embedded journalists in flak jackets and helmets emerged from the shadows, cautiously snapping pictures of rubble or abandoned alleyways before being ushered on by their military escorts. Police and the BOPE had secured most of the complex and the community tentatively opened for business once again. The Morro's brief invasion was over. Police and military congratulated each other on their success.

"Pizzerias, gas stations, hotels are open," tweeted Rene.

There were some arrests and a few casualties. The media that came to capture the violence saw only the remains of military search operations. They filmed a symbolic raising of the Brazilian and Rio state flags on the Complexo do Alemão; a carefully staged PR event that signaled to the world the success of the campaign. But the CV had long since fled with their arsenals to bolt holes in the further reaches of the city.

Rosental Alves, UNESCO Chair in Communication, tweeted his own thoughts in conclusion of the campaign:

"My tribute to Rene Silva's @vozdacomunidade and staff. Founder of the paper 11, a war correspondent at 17."

In the following days, Complexo do Alemão returned to its own version of normality, albeit a slightly edgier one. Children once again flooded the streets and parents took buses to work in the morning. The apartment block of one of the leading drug barons, left empty by his retreat, was opened to the public. Police found a 40" plasma TV and air conditioning. Moleques enjoyed their once-in-a-lifetime party in the penthouse pool, as if the events of the previous days were a world away. Residents were still aware of the permanent specter that hung over them: the prospect of the military withdrawing and leaving it open for the gangs to return and wreak havoc, with reprisals on the community.

"Better days will come!" tweeted Rene. "Rio will continue. We are still going to eat pizza and laugh a lot together."

Favelados know chance blows like a flame in the wind. You could be playing in the street with your neighbors and take a bullet from a stray inter-gang shootout. It may not be election year, so the favelas may not be on the agenda. FIFA, organizers of the World Cup, and the International Olympic Committee could have chosen other countries to host their events. The BOPE may have targeted another favela instead, driving the CV and ADA to your neighborhood. Foreign journalists will leave one day. Investment will dry up in the carousel that is the global economy. Autocrats will be ousted only for more of the same to be ushered in. As with every campaign there is a day when the politicians have to fry bigger fish and leave the Morro to fend for itself. What will happen tomorrow is never known, so when a chance presents itself you take it.

Media had long been the preserve of the elite. Wealthy tycoons bought newspapers and TV stations to extend their power and reach. But now, even a teenager living in a shanty town has all the tools he needs to broadcast his story to the world: a mobile phone and a voice.

"25th November 2010," tweeted one follower, "the day that the community's voice was heard."

10 WEIBO, CHINA

A huddle of suburban skyscrapers hovers above a thick plume of steel-blue smog, like a harbinger of the future. Beneath the cloudy veil, a city moans. Under the shadow of the sleek, functional bridge leading into the city, a 22-year-old street vendor, Lu, hawks iPhone cases and "Roleksu" watches. I stand with my interpreter as Lu enthusiastically waylays foreign tourists.

"He's not greeting you," says the snaggle-toothed vendor to an American couple who make the mistake of catching his eye, "he's waving goodbye."

Lu's watch shows a smiling Mao Tse-tung, replete with waving arms for watch hands. It fails to impress. A lone Scandinavian visitor walks past the stall without acknowledging the vendor.

"See! He's not greeting you..."

Lu's enthusiasm gives way to a resigned expression. He pulls up his stool, tugs up the legs of his pants to catch the sun and lights a Red Pagoda Mountain cigarette. He turns to face the sea to collect his thoughts.

In Mao's era, vendors like Lu would have been forced into the fields to harvest the rice bowl that fuelled China's revolution. Today, his generation have more material wealth and resources than their parents ever dreamt of. It seems appropriate that the grandfather of the revolution should be waving goodbye as the new era arrives. Is this the utopian future that Lu's parents sacrificed everything for?

Behind Lu's stall lies a vast expanse of empty ocean straddled by the Qingdao Haiwan Bridge stretching some 40 kilometers to the south across the Bohai strait. Out of this blue vista once came the Yang Ren (the "ocean people") from Europe brandishing diplomacy through the barrel of a rifle. The invaders crossing the ocean today are no longer foreign, but young people from China's provinces. In the last decade, an estimated 200 million Chinese left their home towns and moved to burgeoning cities like Qingdao in China's North Eastern Shandong province. By most estimates, it's the largest migration in rural history. As Lu sets up his stall every morning, the main roads leading into Qingdao begin to snarl with transit vans and coaches carrying hopeful factory workers, students and runaways escaping the eternal poverty of the countryside. Traffic jams snake back over the bridge, across the bay and are eventually swallowed by the perpetual smog. For those that make the long journey, the city presents countless new opportunities, but the eventual outcomes are often limited to one of two.

The first outcome can be seen on Qingdao's backstreets that echo with the sound of loud-mouthed men and women with sun-blackened faces and unkempt hair. Their harsh voices fill noodle shops like shockwaves of the past. They came to populate the workshops of the world and build its LCD TVs, iPhones and cheap plastic toys. Lucent opened the floodgates when it set up its global manufacturing hub here in 2000. But despite the dot-com bubble having been and gone, the rural migrants that once cascaded through the factory gates still remain. Huddled beneath the weather-beaten tarpaulin of roadside tea-stalls, they stare passively at the city and the mobile future that seems to be passing them by.

The other outcome is seen in the aspirational middle classes who have seized the opportunity created by change. They have been drawn to the city by images of young Chinese living out the consumerist dream with the brazen confidence of New Yorkers. As they gather in the evening, they greet each other with air-kisses and fashion tips, only pausing to send a flurry of mobile phone messages. In this modernist utopia everyone is driven by the sense of urgency and hope, but they carry with them an agitation of the soul. They eat French cheese, drink Scottish whisky and mix Coke with new world red wine, without tradition to hobble their lifestyle.

Lu came to Qingdao on the premise that he'd make enough money in three years to be able to return to Jining and support his extended family. But in his third year, the middle class dream continues to elude him.

"I used to work downtown," explains Lu, "but the police kept moving me on so I'm stuck up here. It's not a great place for business because the kind of people who hang round the bridge are either lost tourists or people from the country. They're not buying watches."

In a staccato rhythm he points out prime trading locations for his stall further up the bay like a general surveying the battlefield for strategic vantage points. Most is talk: Lu's strategies are the stuff of fantasies, plans once made and promises broken.

"Just there, by the college. Over there I have first option on a lease. We're going to build a coffee house. Like Starbucks in New York, but Chinese. All these young people," he says gesturing at the masses, "have money, but nowhere to relax with friends."

He deftly retains a thumb's width of ash at the end of his cigarette while drawing out his plans in the air.

Soon after Lu's arrival in 2008, he felt his course in Agriculture wasn't the right vehicle to maneuver him into China's fast lane. So he set up his own business importing watches and gadgets from Guangzhou. Despite initial success, delays with his suppliers left him short of vital cash flow and he was left unable to source the stock that the more discerning youth of modern China wanted. No more Gucci knock-offs. No more iPhone cases. But there was one thing Lu had an abundance of, like so many in his generation – optimism. He still had several palate loads of O'Neill sunglasses and last year's supply of Kappa watches: the bellwethers of his trade. As he stares out across the water to uptown Qingdao his optimism makes you feel like his moment is just around the corner. The rising tide of China's economy has raised many boats. Despite the prevailing wisdom favoring meritocracy, many still believe, like Lu, in being in the right place at the right time.

It's the end of the October National Holiday and Lu has co-opted a local sweet potato trader's spot further up the bay to ply his wares.

"This will be a good week," Lu speculates. "They'll be buying stuff to take back to their home towns. A watch is as good a gift as any. When I sell this crate, I'll have enough money to set up my coffee house. Look! Genuine Louis Vuitton replicas."

But business passes him by. He seems too pre-occupied with messages on his mobile phone to engage a group of young couples who hold hands, talk on their phones and eat cotton candy, whilst hovering around his stall trying on the sunglasses in front of a small mirror hanging by a wire from the stall's canopy. In this new era of self-expression, flirting teenagers have replaced stiff-suited banqueting bureaucrats as young Qingdao parades its latest fashions and technologies by the waterfront.

After three days of hanging out with Lu, his patter softens from the bravado of business to the vulnerability of romance.

"I'd go back to Jining any day," he says, from shade of his accessories stall. "I don't like my apartment on the 14th floor. The elevator never works and is always full of junk. I miss the old courtyards of my home town. Here I have to lock the door even when I'm in. The place smells of piss. Who pisses in their own hallway? Immigrants and dogs, that's who," he explains, somehow conveniently forgetting he's not long off the Haiwan Bridge himself. "And besides, I can't go home single. My parents will bully me into finding a local girl, but I don't want that. I don't want a country girl. Look at this one," Lu says while brandishing a profile of a girl on his phone. Lu's expression soon lightens. "She looks like a model, but you have to be careful. At the bottom it says 'I'm looking for a man who can also take care of my mother'," he laughs, gesturing as if swatting imaginary flies around him. "Pah... pah... go away... I left all that behind in Jining."

He stares back at the screen of his phone and speedily dispatches a short message before snapping back to our conversation.

"How do you hope to meet the right girl?" I ask.

"Here? No. This is no place to meet a girl. They don't come down here. Mobile phone, maybe. I'm trying to find one on my mobile phone. This one, she's gorgeous. We've already exchanged phone numbers."

Lu shows me his phone again.

"Little Nana has just turned 19. Qingnong female, studying foreign language at Qingdao Agricultural University, born in 1992, 162 centimeters tall, home town is Jining in Shandong Provence, has the loveliness of an eastern northerner. Looking for a university freshman, sophomore, or junior around the height of 176–183 cm, slim, and doesn't have to be too handsome as this isn't the most important thing, it's more important that we hit it off."

Lu sees the look on my face and his smile slowly breaks into laughter. I'm not sure if he's serious or joking. I think it's more the former, mixed with a degree of humor to relieve the pressure of the situation. I stare at Lu's nicotine-stained gapped teeth and wonder what Little Nana would make of this roguish migrant who gave up his university education for a watch stand. The viability of this romance is, perhaps, a joke that Lu is in on himself. On the one hand he sees the irony of the mismatch between Little Nana's needs and his own situation, but on the other he appears hardened to his distinct lack of attractiveness.

"Not real," he says, once again throwing up a smokescreen to protect his own vulnerabilities. "See, she's just a girl on the mobile phone. Not real."

Lu then dismisses the conversation, kissing his teeth as he pulls up his knee-high stool ready for some real business at his stall. He looks disappointed with my gullibility; for not believing the whole Little Nana story was a joke.

But was it a joke? Lu's path to romance is a mobile messaging service popular in China called Weibo. Weibo, much like an extended version of Twitter, is a mobile messaging app favored by young Chinese that was initially tolerated by the Communist Party. The logic was that by bringing the conversations of 500 million young Chinese out into the open there would be no more hushed tones in smoky noodle bars or campus cafes. Everything could now be measured and recorded. While Weibo was a private service, the government permitted its use because it didn't have the subversive nature of Facebook, which was also private but, more importantly, foreign.

Weibo soon filled the hole in the social fabric left to a generation without a legacy of connecting. Not wanting to miss the opportunity to gain a foothold in the Weibo community, authorities found the technology to be a useful tool to push their civil society agenda. There were countless stories of young Chinese who fell through the net, disappeared or ended up as beggars in underpasses or night workers in Amo bars. Perhaps Weibo could help to identify and rescue these lost citizens. This was the start of a grassroots Weibo campaign that convinced users to post 1,000 photographs of missing persons. Chen Shiqu, head of the Child Abduction Office at the Public Security Bureau gave his public approval. Within two weeks, 154,000 people were using the service. Party officials lent vocal support to a service that would normally have been treated with suspicion.

Young people got on the rescue bandwagon all right, but not as Shiqu had intended. While the missing persons service became popular, it was not as popular as the unofficial rescue service where young Chinese sought to rescue each other from a life of loneliness, devoid of romance. University Weibo groups began cropping up for the sole purpose of taking the chit-chat and news sharing offline.

"She needs rescuing," posted one young suitor on Little Nana's profile.

"I can rescue her," commented another, "but I'm looking for a taller girl 165 cm+."

In the absence of free services that encouraged unmonitored interaction between youth, Weibo had become, by accident, the default dating service for young Chinese. These weren't dissidents corrupting the regime or strays who had fallen off the map, but youth who were lost in an altogether different sense.

In the many spare hours afforded to Lu at his stall, he has ample time to explore Qingdao's female market stall. And the pressure is on. China's one child policy has created a population with more males than females: there are 120 Lu's for every 100 Nanas. Little Nana's profile amassed 3,200 views, but Lu is ever hopeful that he has something unique to offer. And, if it doesn't work out, love in her many guises is just around the corner.

"Sure, I'm not a freshman anymore, but I was," says Lu. "I told her I was working the stall during the holiday so I could fund my MBA. Okay, it's not totally honest, but this world moves fast. I might meet her tomorrow, but she wants to meet uptown in a restaurant and I haven't got back to her with a better idea. This is modern China: if you don't like what you see, move on."

We talk about whether Lu thinks his generation is any happier than that of his parents and whether technology has improved his outlook. I ask about Xiao Zheng who sold his kidney for an iPad. Lu contemplates whilst taking a deep drag of his cigarette, his head disappearing into a thick cloud of smoke. He pauses and smiles, shaking his head.

"We have money, freedom and more choices. But every night we go back to our one-bedroom apartments and sleep on a mattress on the floor. Alone. Sure, you look at the advertising on TV and we look successful. We have clothes, food and homes but you can say we are a selfish generation. We have more than my parents ever had but we grow up in a world of strangers. That makes us selfish. Happier? I don't know. For my generation, happiness is what comes next, after we have achieved a career and a family. Career, family then happiness. That's why stories like Xiao Zheng's don't mean anything to us. We have other things to think about. But we have the ability to change. The government will, some day, change. It's changing already. Young people have new ideas. There will be a time in the future when we'll say 'enough money, how about some time off with my friends?' That's when Lu opens his coffee house."

Career, family then happiness. I often hear these words spoken in this order in developing markets like China and wonder if this is how they feel deep down. This is the widely accepted public face, but inside China's 500 million young people there's a gnawing sense of unease. They turn to their mobile phones in search of a solution. Perhaps it's career, family and happiness. Why wait?

There is an often cited joke that says if you look at China on TV, it's a harmonious world, but on the internet, it's on the verge of revolution. Perhaps what unites the voices of the mobile generation is this arrow of change.

The author William Gibson wrote, "the future is already here, it's just not evenly distributed," and this is true when we see how youth today use technology.

From Riyadh to Long Island to Beijing, this generation grows up not knowing material hardship. Where their forebears fought for land to grow food and other basic privileges this generation are fighting for something a lot more subtle – space to meet, space to play, space to belong – and technology has become their weapon of choice. Youth starved of space to interact will evolve technologies that help them broadcast their stories and feelings to a world unbound by geography. We all stand to benefit from this arrow of change. From Facebook to text messaging to changing business models, we are already benefitting. The emotional struggles of youth today will become the everyday behaviors of the mass market tomorrow.

ABOUT GRAHAM BROWN

Since witnessing the growth of youth media and technology having lived in Japan in the early 90s, Graham along with business partner Josh Dhaliwal has helped grow mobileYouth to serve over 250 clients in 60 countries worldwide – names such as Vodafone, Nokia, Coke, McDonald's, Telenor, Orange, O2, Verizon, Boost Mobile, the UK government and the European Commission.

Graham is a regular public speaker and has presented at the 3GSM World Congress, Barcelona and been interviewed on CNN, CNBC, BBC TV and Radio. His work has also featured in the Wall Street Journal, Financial Times and the Guardian. He hosts the youth marketing stream on Upstart Radio and mobileYouth's own TV channel.

Graham is also a judge on the Mobile Marketing Association's Award Panel, advisory board member to UNICEF on their mobile media strategies and an advisor to the Global Youth Marketing Forum in India.

www.GrahamDBrown.com
www.mobileYouth.org

Printed in Great Britain
by Amazon.co.uk, Ltd.,
Marston Gate.

The Mobile Youth
voices of the mobile generation

Graham Brown

ISBN: 1480024341
ISBN-13: 978-1480024342